K.tReed

DMC

Cross Stitch
COLOUR BY COLOUR

More Than 100
Exquisite Designs

Designs by Miky Dessein

Photography by Elio Michelotti

Text by Elda Fillippa and Mariarosa Schiaffino

CASSELL

CONTENTS

Published in the UK 1995
by Cassell
Wellington House
125 Strand
London
WC2R OBB

First published in Italy in 1992
by Idealibri s.t.l., Milan, Italy as
Dollfus Mieg & Company: Punto Croce—Sul filo del colore

Copyright © original Italian edition Idealibri s.t.l. 1992
Original text by Elda Filippa

The editor would like to thank Rakam magazine for its part in making this book possible.

Copyright © English language text Hodder Headline Australia Pty Ltd
Translation by Marietta Rossetto
Craft Consultant: Alison Snepp

British Library Cataloguing-in-Publication Data
A catalogue record for this book is available from the British Library

ISBN 0-304-34578-4

All photographs were taken at Romantek Hotel, Turm at Fiè allo Sciliar (Bolzano) and in the Maison Rose at Eugénie-les Bains (France)

Printed and bound in China

INTRODUCTION

Cross stitch, always one of the most popular forms of embroidery, has lately gained an even larger following of embroiders who have taken this form of creativity in hand—literally. This recent surge of interest may be due in a large part to the fact that while the technique itself is relatively easy to master, the results can be breathtaking.

DMC, a name in the field for over two centuries and a world leader in embroidery, has responded to the 'desire to embroider' by undertaking a series of initiatives which has had important results. One such initative is their long collaboration with Rakam—the prestigious magazine in Italy promoting handicrafts—which has contributed in a decisive way to the diffusion of interest in embroidery.

Cross stitch holds a prominent position as a craft form—its freshness, simplicity and appeal of subject matter have been, and are, winning attractions.

Even with the hectic pace of today's lifestyle, would-be embroiders will find it an easy and enjoyable craft. Most projects are of a size that is easily portable—allowing you to stitch at various moments during the day—and even a few minutes' work each day will yield a finished piece in a surprisingly short time.

Colour plays a major role in determining the beauty of an embroidered piece, so the chapters of this book have been divided by colour—and great care has been given to the choice of threads for each project to ensure stunning results.

Whether a beginner or an experienced cross stitcher, DMC Cross Stitch: Colour by Colour will be the perfect cross stitch resource that will be referred to for years to come as a limitless source of design inspiration.

Dollfus Mieg & Co.

FABRIC

Zweigart Aida or linen
Fabric is often referred to by threads or stitches per inch. The table below will help you in obtaining the fabrics you need to complete any of the projects featured in this book.

STITCH COUNT PER 10CM	STITCH COUNT PER INCH (over two threads when worked on linen)
72	18
60	16
55	14
44	11

PREFACE

"If you know how to sew on a button you know how to embroider a rose." Whoever formulated such an encouraging assertion must have been referring to cross stitch. This book aims to prove the truth of this assertion.

A cross stitch is a tiny, tiny stitch with widespread fame today. It is a form of embroidery that requires simple patience and yet gives extraordinary results. It can also be learnt from the pages of this book. Cross stitch is a temptation that is difficult to resist because its main appeal stems from its 'scholastic method' approach which sets out the instructions in a manner that ensures easy, accurate mastery of the necessary skills.

In the past, experienced needleworkers were available to pass on their skills to beginners within the home environment. There existed an oral tradition of easy, spontaneous words and gestures through which the craft was taught in the calmer moments of the day.

Today, must we renounce this tradition because life is too hectic and rushed? No. This book aims to encourage cross stitch, which is easier to discover and rediscover than one might imagine. Cross stitch is not only a wonderfully meditative history, but it also provides a satisfying link with our past. The chapters in this book lay out the beautiful story of embroidery enhanced by scintillating colours and subtle shading. The glorious photographs and carefully selected design graphs will inspire your creativity.

We are convinced that the revival of this craft will be a story with a happy ending.

Anna Gualteri
Director of Rakam

COLOUR HARMONY
IN CROSSED THREADS

Traditionally, white is the colour of household linen. Colour, however, has always been used to brighten and enliven home decor. Colour also plays a leading role in cross stitch.

Cross stitch is a technique that was the most popular and widely used embroidery stitch of the last century. This genial craft was first used in Germany in 1804 and contributed, in a very significant fashion, to the development of associated stitches such as the Continental stitch, half stitch and tent stitch. Today, cross stitch is enjoying a renewed popularity so vast that it is considered a 'phenomenon' at the centre of the revival of traditional handicrafts, in general, and embroidery, in particular. The reasons for this revival probably lie in the easy execution of the craft and its extremely appealing decorative impact.

Cross stitch is easier to do than to say. It is geometrical, regular and simple to follow, and it uses the fabric count of loosely woven material such as canvas. You simply work twice in diagonal directions, crossing one stitch over the other. It is sometimes called square stitch because of this basic structure and also because cross stitch designs are usually drawn on to graph paper—every square represents a stitch,

making the precision of the craft extremely easy to master and original designs, faces and motifs easy to create.

With colour and tone it is possible to create greater clarity of designs and a three-dimensional effect similar to that of tapestry. In needlework dating from the seventeenth and eighteenth centuries, the shadings of the colour are, generally speaking, more subdued. This is not solely due to fading over time as, back then, there was a widespread interest in light colours—the harmony and effect of tone on tone or on a number of restricted tints gave a very refined look to decorations—but, in the nineteenth century, especially in the second half, the discovery of aniline dye, which was used in the industrial world to dye yarn, created a whole range of tints which were much richer in tone. This change in colour appreciation spread to embroidery, and the craft adopted the use of stronger colours and contrasts which were a far cry from the tonal qualities of the previous century.

Today, naturally, chemical advances and nature itself provide us with an infinite array of yarns and threads of various colours and tints. A wider range of colours now makes almost any design possible. A few base

colours, or one colour in various tones, or, in a completely opposite manner, a multitude of tints and gradations can be used to give a masterly shading or a particular effect to an embroidered piece.

This book has chosen to highlight the theme of coloured thread—from rose to green, from yellow to blue, to red, to violet, to orange—and the array offers a myriad of ideas and suggestions.

We have developed the theme of colour liberally, encompassing flowering vine shoots and garlands, baskets of fruit, bunches of flowers tied with ribbons and, embracing the classical notion of the garden, the vegetable patch, the orchard and the countryside. This aspect of nature is an inspirational theme of the embroidery motif. There are also other traditional motifs in cross stitch that have been reinterpreted in modern style: the letters of the alphabet and the numbers used in samplers or in beginners' works on which the young embroiderer learn the art of sewing as well as the skills of reading, writing and arithmetic. Geometric and stylised motifs are presented as centre pieces, borders, and frames offering another outlet for the creative self and personal initiative.

The photographed works are set out in planned designs which are easy to follow—sometimes a single motif, but more often, a repeated pattern forming a border. Many additional designs on various themes are set out in chart form only. Another significant feature of the designs is that, for each, instructions are given with details of the number of stitches required and the measurements according to the type of fabric chosen. This information is extremely practical for anyone about to begin embroidery because the actual dimensions are already calculated and the process of adapting a design is clearly explained.

Therefore you can choose the stitches, the season and the desired colour of thread. Our wish is that cross stitch will be for you as it was for the passionate devotee who claimed that "Embroidery is happiness created".

Mariarosa Schiaffino

Inspirations in
ROSE

*O*ptimism, confidence, benevolence, sweetness—no other colour evokes such a positive vision of life as the rose coloured thread used in embroidery. The statistics confirm this: In dinner settings for the table, in personal linen, and in the bathroom, rose is the favourite choice of colour worldwide.

A calm colour, born of the mixture of red (aggressive and dynamic) with white (innocent and peaceful), it gathers the striking clarity of the former by warming the coolness of the latter.

There is no aspect of this colour that can be viewed negatively. It is the aura of dreams, love stories and tenderness. Even nature expresses its most gentle and benign self through the colour rose—the flush of a baby's cheeks, the fullness of a peach, the transparent coral *pelle d'angelo*, the exquisite flesh of salmon and shrimp.

The finest creation of the colour rose is the beautiful flower, queen of the gardens, which takes its name from the colour (or is it vice versa?) and displays it in all its most enchanting shades. The floral world is bursting with pink: the magnificent peony, the subtle azalea, the gentle periwinkle (clematis), the wild heather and a thousand other species. It is for this reason that the colour rose is featured so often in embroidery: corollas, buds, rosy petals spread across the linen, gathering close in bunches and cascading in garlands.

$\mathcal{A}$bove and detailed on page 11: The floral border is the undisputed central feature of cross stitch embroidery. It is the 'patchwork motif' normally indicated on a design with letters or arrows. Most patchworks include a border that is useful for decorating long strips such as the edge of a sheet, the outer edge of a quilt, the bottom of a curtain, or the edge of a tablecloth. On this border, the toned colours merge into the clear woven surface of the fabric which is almost an antique white.

$\mathcal{R}$ight: These little square gardens enhance a tablecloth and are linked together with a white latticework decorated with a subtle green creeper. This combination can decorate the table surface and the fall of the tablecloth, and can have countless variations because there are no limits to geometric possibilities—chess board patterns, zigzags, diagonal designs and so on.. It is always best to plan the design before beginning, sketching it out in proportion on graph paper with precise measurements.

*L*eft: To speak of cross stitch without referring to samplers, or first attempts, is overlooking the full story. This is a delightful first attempt with a delicate union of initials and numbers, flowers around the border, and non-geometric shapes—almost an album of designs that can be consulted when looking for inspiration for a picture frame, a finishing touch or a border (See pp. 24–25)

*A*bove: Another border design which makes ingenious use of the bands of cross stitch passing under the nosegays and linking them together to give life to this very beautiful American design. Light yellow (or another pale colour) can be used for the bands; soft pastel tones ranging from rose to red, green or light blue for the flowers. Note that the more you increase the number of squares per 10 centimetres, the smaller the embroidery design. (See pp. 22–23 and p. 98.)

*A*bove and right: A tavern-style checked tablecloth with a difference. Choose a chic colour like grey for the fabric. For the flowers and leaves, use the full range of the deeper shades of rose and sprinkle the green with yellow. Vary the flowers. Use cross stitch for the blooms, outlining in backstitch, and contrast this with the flower motifs in backstitch only.

Inspirations in Rose
THE DESIGNS

*The colour numbers of all the designs in this book
refer to the DMC Stranded cotton.

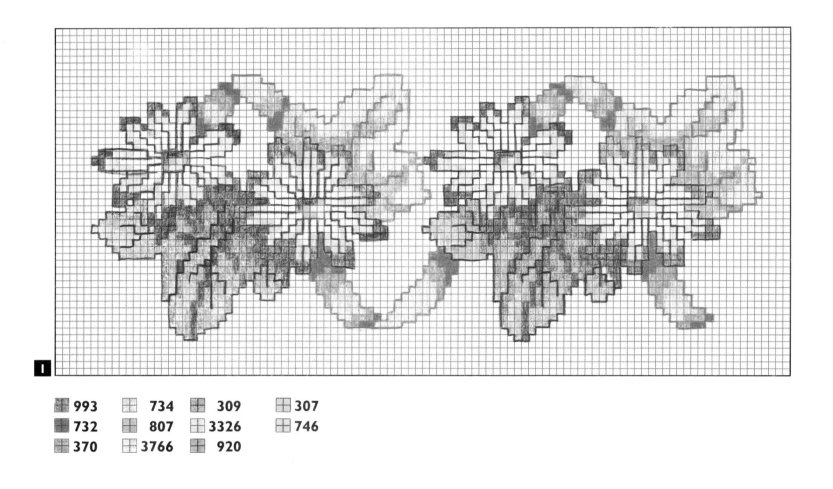

1

▦	993	⊞	734	▦	309	⊞	307
▦	732	⊞	807	⊞	3326	⊞	746
▦	370	⊞	3766	▦	920		

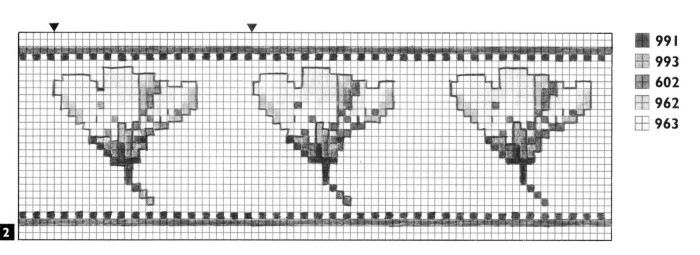

2

▪	991
⊞	993
▦	602
⊞	962
⊞	963

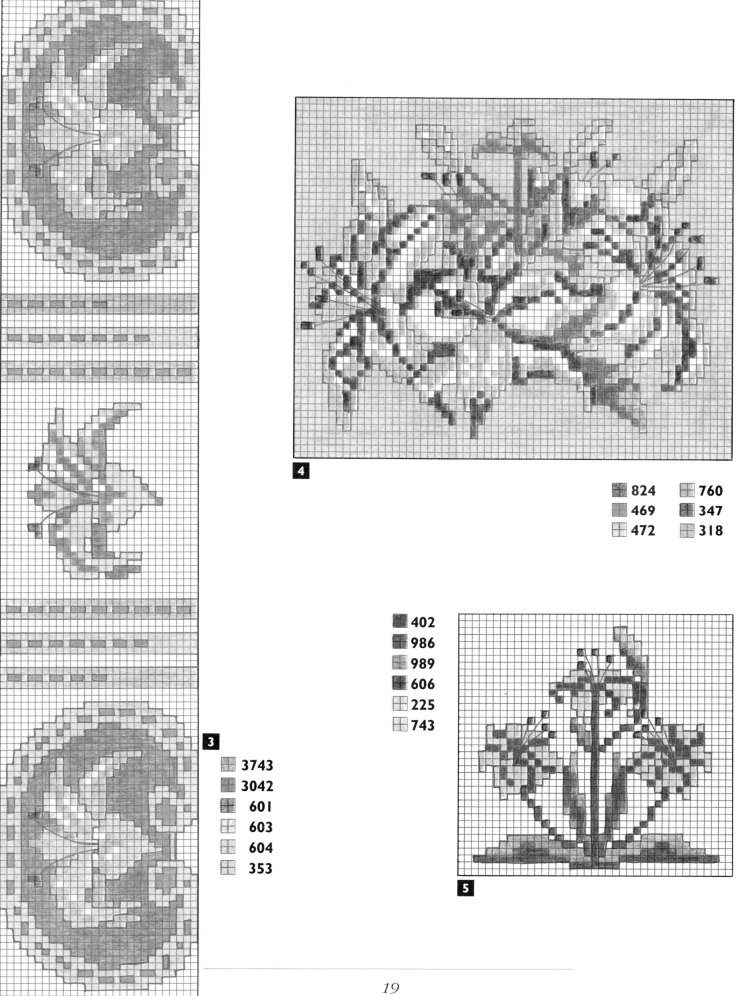

4

	824		760
	469		347
	472		318

3

	3743
	3042
	601
	603
	604
	353

	402
	986
	989
	606
	225
	743

5

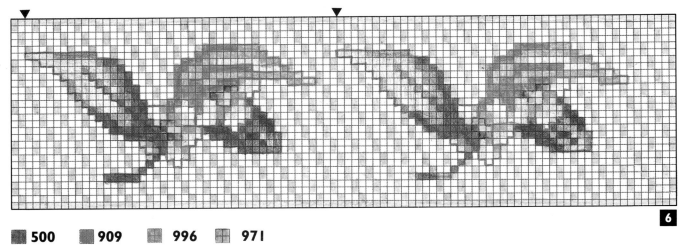

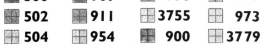

■ 500	■ 909	⊞ 996	⊞ 971	
⊞ 502	⊞ 911	⊞ 3755	⊞ 973	
⊞ 504	⊞ 954	⊞ 900	⊞ 3779	

6

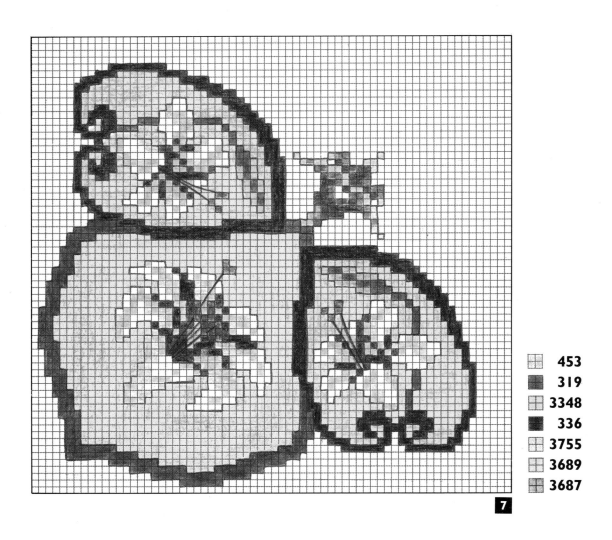

⊞	453
■	319
⊞	3348
■	336
⊞	3755
⊞	3689
⊞	3687

7

8

⊞	**778**	⊞	**827**	⊞	**907**
⊞	**3687**	⊞	**824**	⊞	**986**
⊞	**453**				

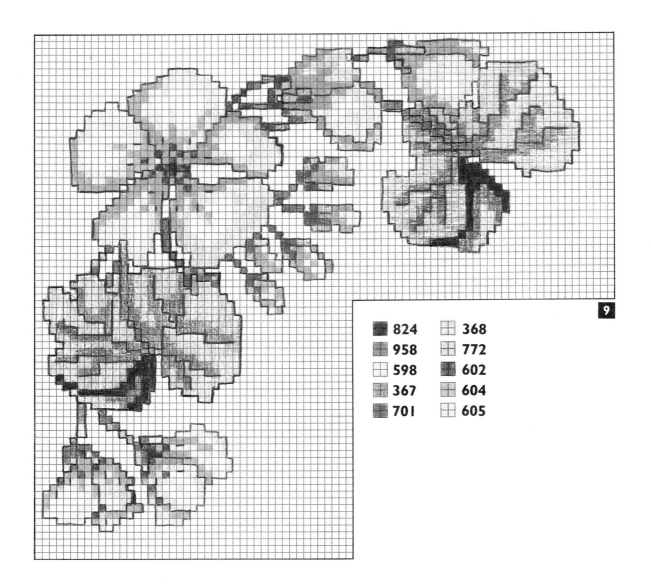

9

■	824	⊞	368
■	958	⊞	772
⊞	598	■	602
▦	367	⊞	604
■	701	⊞	605

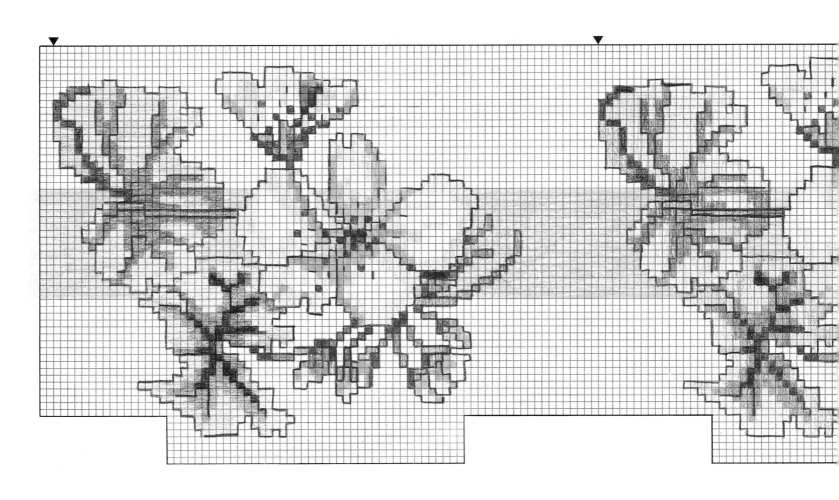

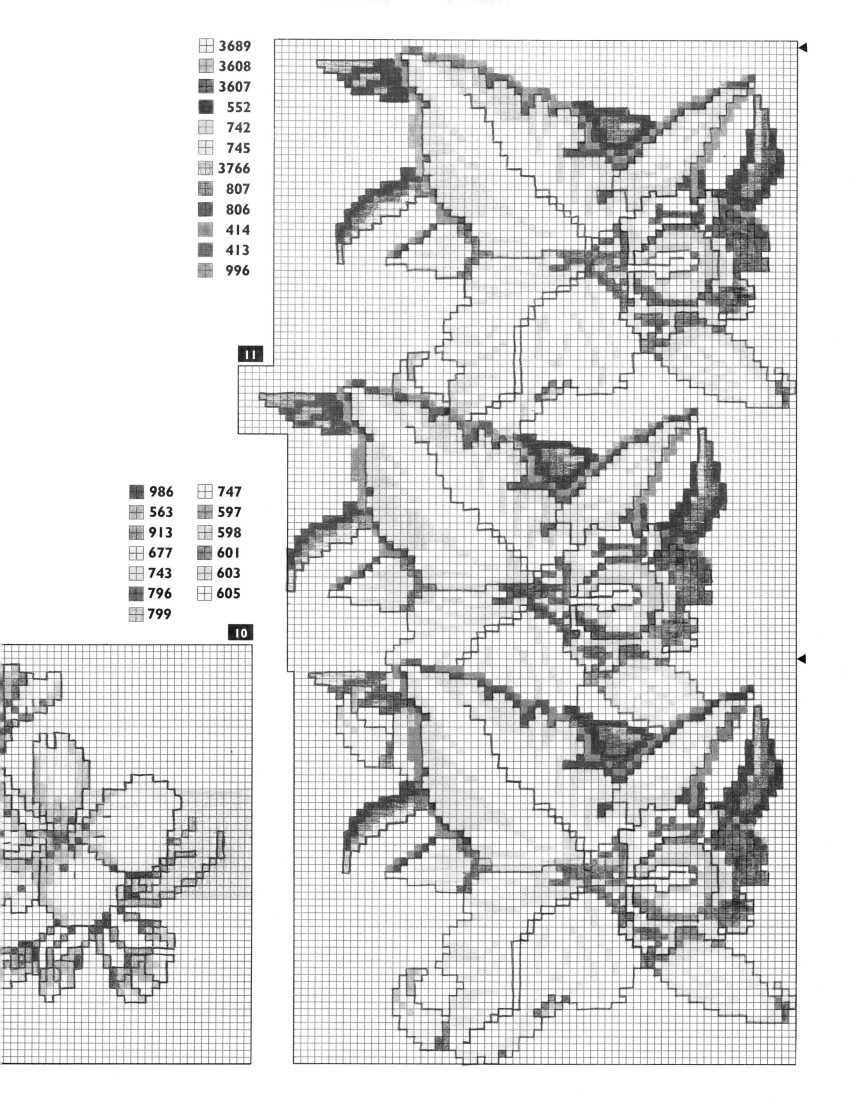

3689
3608
3607
552
742
745
3766
807
806
414
413
996

11

986   747
563   597
913   598
677   601
743   603
796   605
799

10

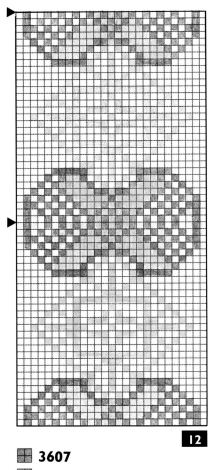

12

3607
3608
3609
945

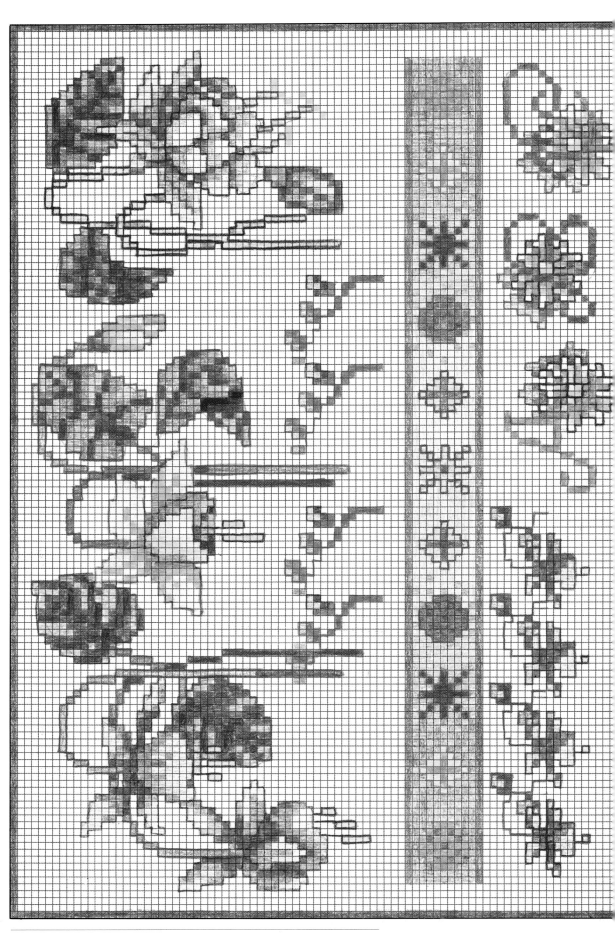

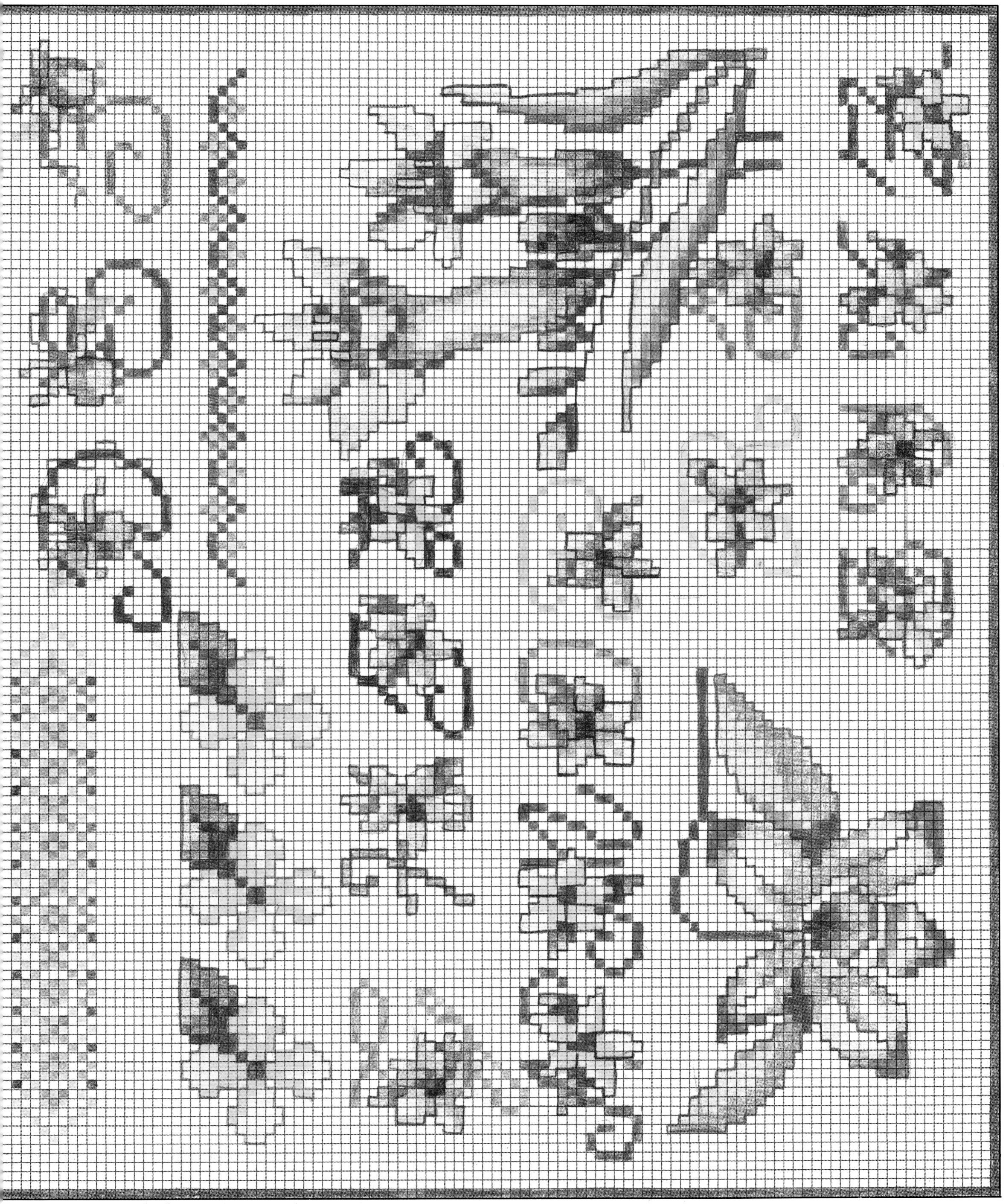

- 666
- 727
- 726
- 725
- 783
- 780
- 3341
- 3340
- 946
- 3733
- 3731
- 601
- 351
- 603
- 554
- 552
- 550
- 209
- 208
- 211
- 3608
- 3607
- 3609
- 564
- 563
- 562
- 991
- 993
- 772
- 472
- 702
- 733
- 580
- 807
- 806
- 341
- 3746

13

Inspirations in
BLUE

$\mathcal{T}$he sky and sea are immense blue expanses that surround us and calm our souls. Blue's diversity is seen in the light wispy colours of a foggy morning to the dark mysterious depths of the ocean. We also draw a sense of freshness, serenity and order from this colour, sometimes tinged with the haunting melancholy of the deeper tones of Blues music.

When we wear it, blue can represent youthfulness, a sporty feeling like the universality of jeans; or, on more formal occasions, it can denote the seriousness, security and elegance of a suit. It is even a symbol of nobility as it is said that 'blue blood' flows in the veins of aristocrats.

Blue entered the world of the arts—especially the handicrafts such as mosaics, stained glass and ceramics where it attained unparalleled fame—from China. When the porcelain of the so called 'blue family' arrived in Europe, it captured the enthusiasm and passion of many. All the large European manufacturing companies adopted blue, often making it the preferred colour—the Dutch with Delft, the Danish with Royal Copenhagen, the French with Limoges, the English with Wedgwood and the Portuguese with Azulejos. Even today, table settings and decorative items in blue tones, from the most exquisite porcelain to the most casual ceramics, have undisputed popularity.

As a result of tradition and revival trends, blue has a special place in embroidery—alongside white, it takes on a special lightness; combined with gold, blue assumes an exceptional preciousness. In both country and city homes one finds a fresh, eternal vitality in the blue motifs featured against the whiteness of cotton and linen.

On page 27: A true classic which perfectly imitates ceramics pieces with a motif reproduced at regular intervals. This repetition makes it possible to lengthen or shorten the design as desired. The beautiful mirror image of the corners creates a pleasing symmetry. You can frame an entire tablecloth, or simply decorate down one side in the American style, or along the bottom edge of a curtain. For maximum stylish effect, embroider the bottom of the border in cross stitch; an easy task because the lines fill up quickly and effortlessly.

Left: This sampler is a return to tradition. The many tones of blue accentuate the splendour of an impeccable piece of workmanship. The crosses create areas of shade and light, and the sampler is suggestive of an extra-ordinary wall panel, a picture that needs no frame. (See pp. 44–45)

Above: This border motif is repeated to frame a group of four little blue swallows. This design makes use of just a few colour tones and develops in a linear fashion with the motif pattern repeated on the same line. If the frame seems too narrow, try doubling it, repeating the mirror motif on the outside. (See pp. 36 and 40)

*L*eft: This traditional floret runner creates a multipurpose border, perfect for a frame, on the edge of a sheet, or on lots of coloured cushions to complement an all-white bed. This pattern also creates an impression of depth. First embroider the flowers and then, with perfect regularity, work the background. The final result will be richer, more defined and very stylish if delicate contrasting tones such as rose and blue are chosen. (See p. 20)

*A*bove: Just as sideboard cupboards are increasing in popularity, so too are antique border patterns. They can be changed from shelf to shelf to highlight colours and classic designs such as blue porcelain. Here is a tip on how to check what the border motif will look like as a corner: place a mirror on the diagonal of the motif so that it reflects its image. The combination of the motif and the reflected image will indicate the possibilities of the design.

*L*eft: This piece has the appearance of a tray made of fine blue porcelain. It is a wonderful design for a beautiful centrepiece to complement your accessories. Measure the size of your favourite tray— perhaps the one used each morning for breakfast—to gauge the size you will need to make the finished embroidery. It will be an elegant and cultured way to begin the day. (See pp. 46–47)

*A*bove: The stylish little centre flower from the 'tray' opposite can be lifted to create a charming little bag. On a blue-grey background dotted with white, the mofit has the appearance of a large, rich medallion. The plotted Aida border with a white base is folded in two and is reminiscent of the fresh decor of the twenties. Remember: on Aida fabric of 72 stitches per 10 cm, the flower is roughly 4.5 x 6 cm. On 44 stitches per 10 cm, it is approximately 7.5 x 9 cm.

*O*pposite: The peony on its own can decorate a chair or a footstool to achieve a striking effect. The single flower without leaves requires 76 x 78 stitches. On Aida fabric of 44 stitches per 10 cm, the flower measures roughly 17 x 18 cm. It is most important, for a good result, to centre the design on the fabric. Mark the centre of the chart and the centre of the fabric. Begin to embroider from the centre.

*A*bove: The large flower, shaded in the softest tones, is a gentle peony that begs to be swirled in blue to resemble the colour of clouds. For an exceptional tablecloth, one flower in each corner of the cloth is sufficient. The woven effect is obtained by working small stripes at regular intervals on the drop of the cloth. A variation would be to embroider two flowers in the centre and then complete the rest of the table square in the woven design.

THE DESIGNS

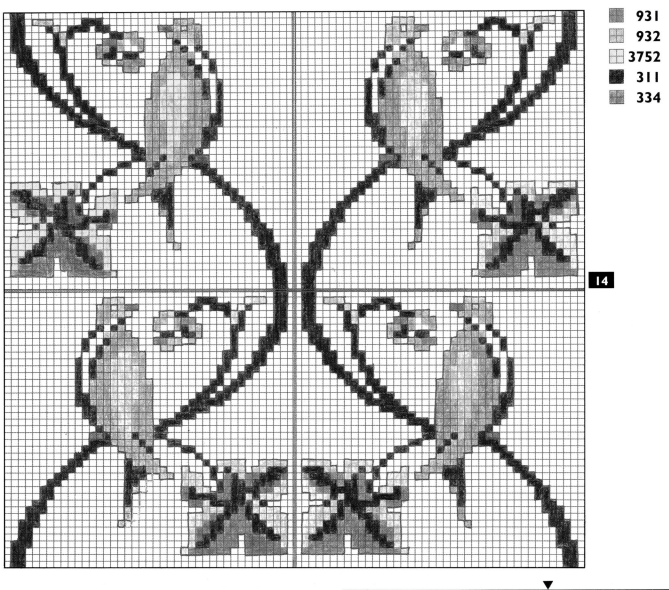

■	931
▦	932
▦	3752
■	311
▦	334

14

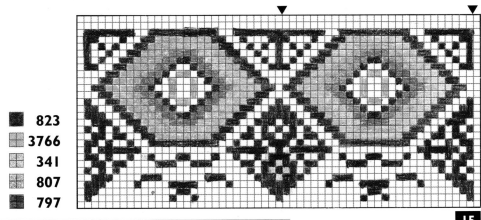

■	823
▦	3766
▦	341
▦	807
■	797

15

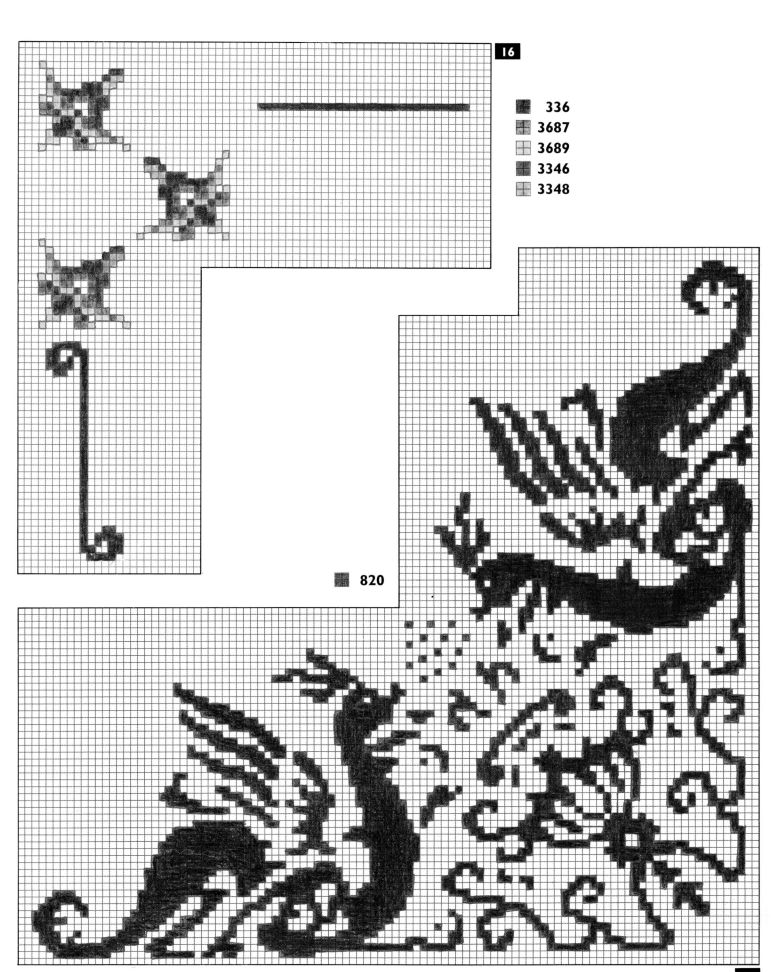

336
3687
3689
3346
3348

820

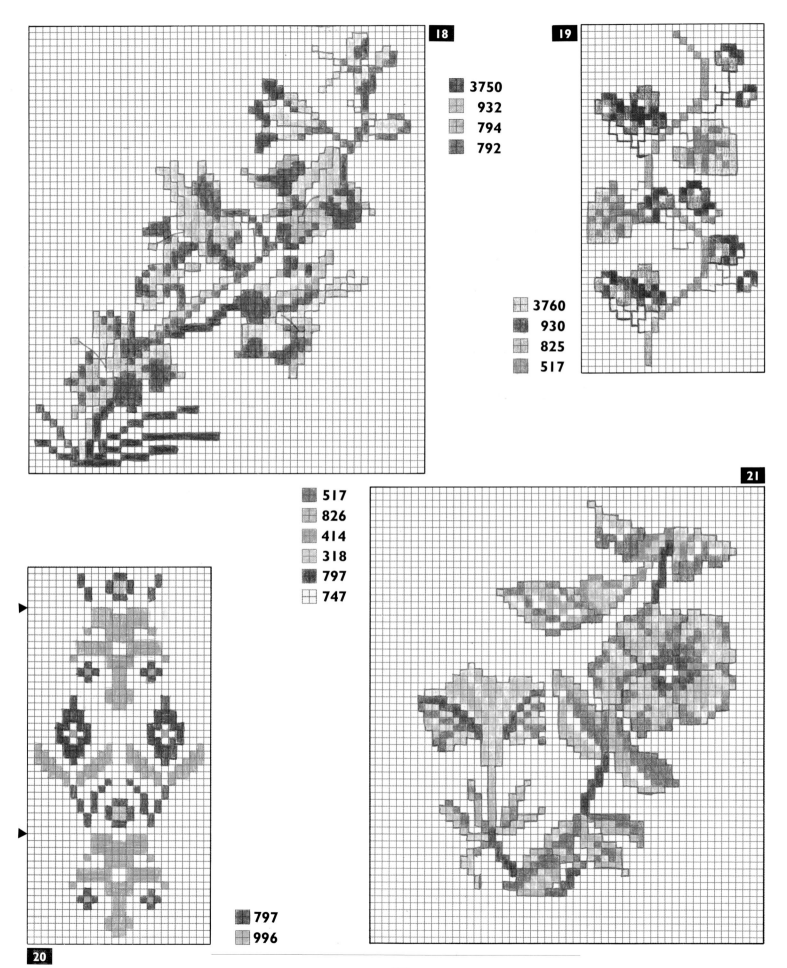

18

■ 3750
▦ 932
▦ 794
▦ 792

19

▦ 3760
▦ 930
▦ 825
▦ 517

■ 517
▦ 826
▦ 414
▦ 318
■ 797
⊞ 747

21

■ 797
▦ 996

20

22

■ 797	⊞ 775		
■ 3760	⊞ 3756		
⊞ 3325			

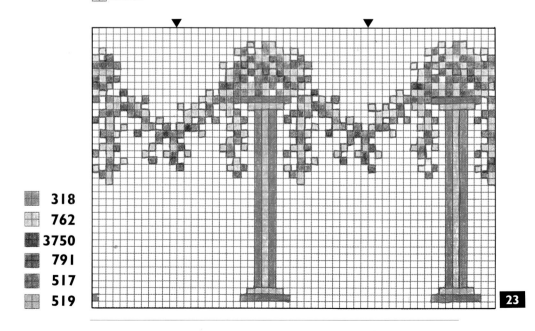

■ 318
⊞ 762
■ 3750
■ 791
■ 517
■ 519

23

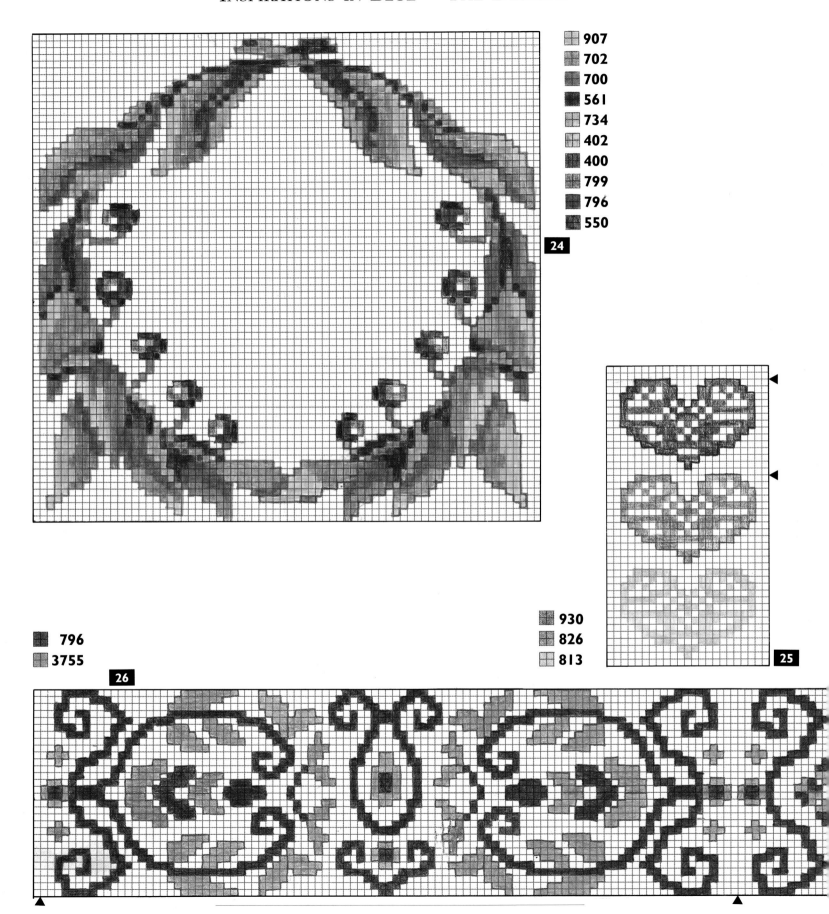

907
702
700
561
734
402
400
799
796
550

24

930
826
813

25

796
3755

26

27

- 3765
- 791
- 794
- 931
- 932

28

930

29

30

312
3755

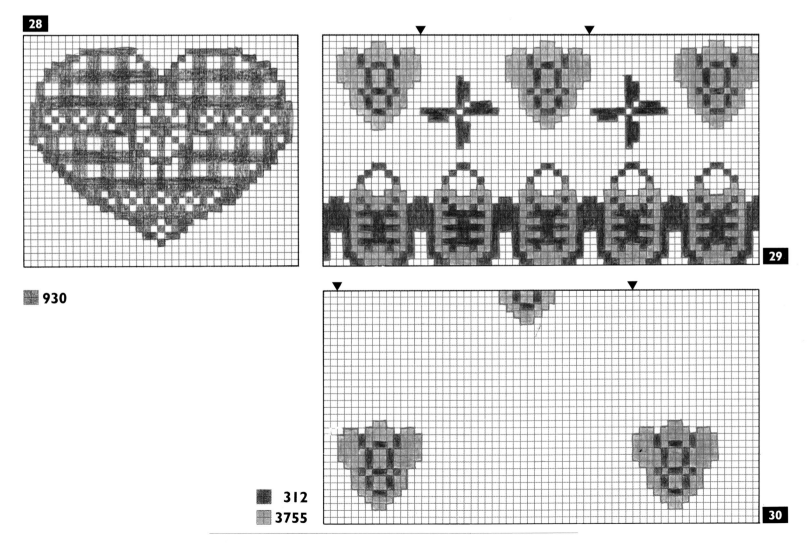

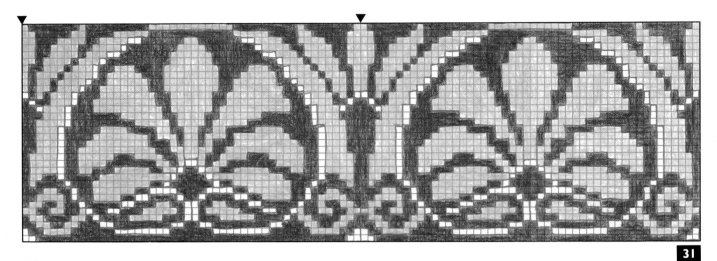

31

■ 312
▦ 3753

32

▦ 823

▦ 813
■ 824

33

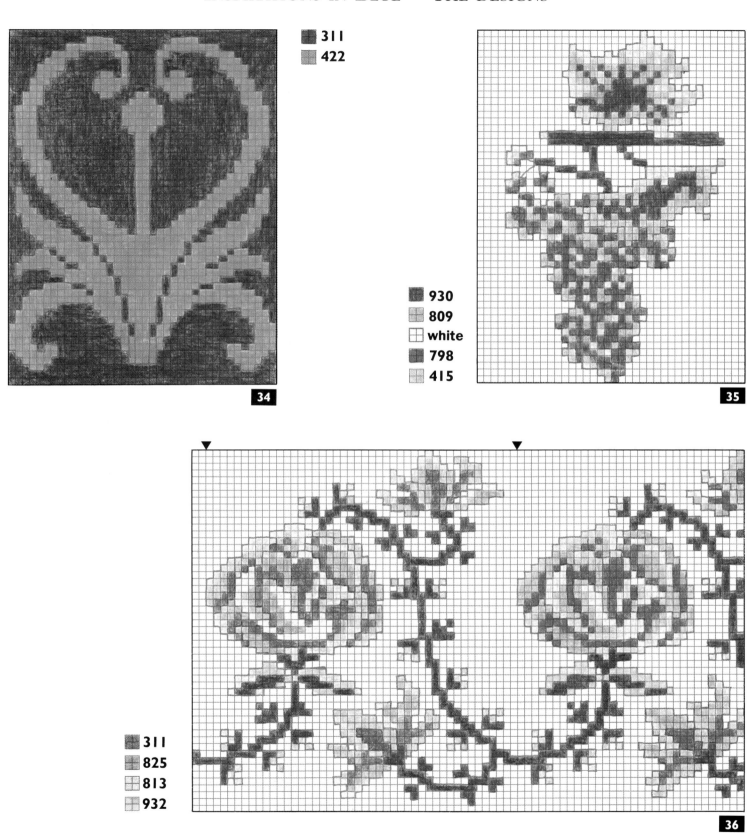

■ 311
▩ 422

34

■ 930
▩ 809
⊞ white
■ 798
▩ 415

35

▩ 311
▩ 825
⊞ 813
▩ 932

36

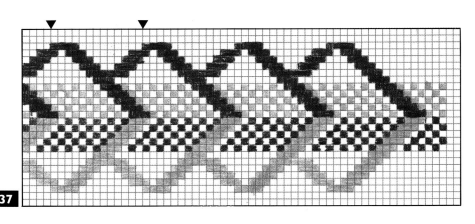

37

■ 311
■ 334
■ 3325

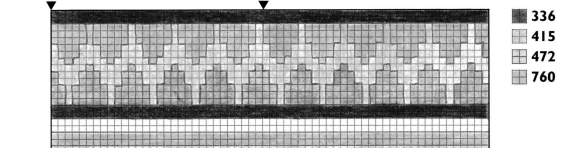

38

■ 336   ■ 3328
■ 469   ■ 760
■ 472   ■ 762

■ 336
□ 415
□ 472
□ 760

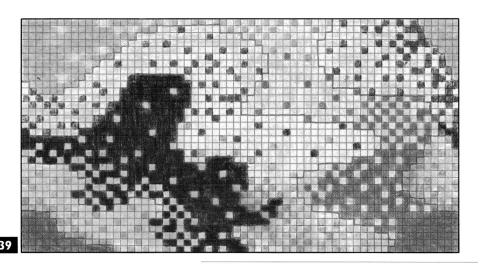

39

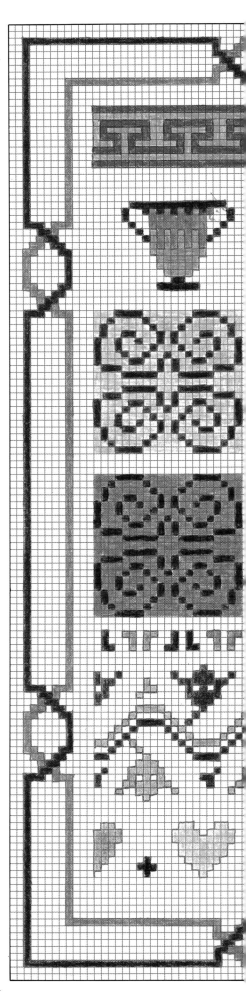

798
3765
807
824
826
762
414

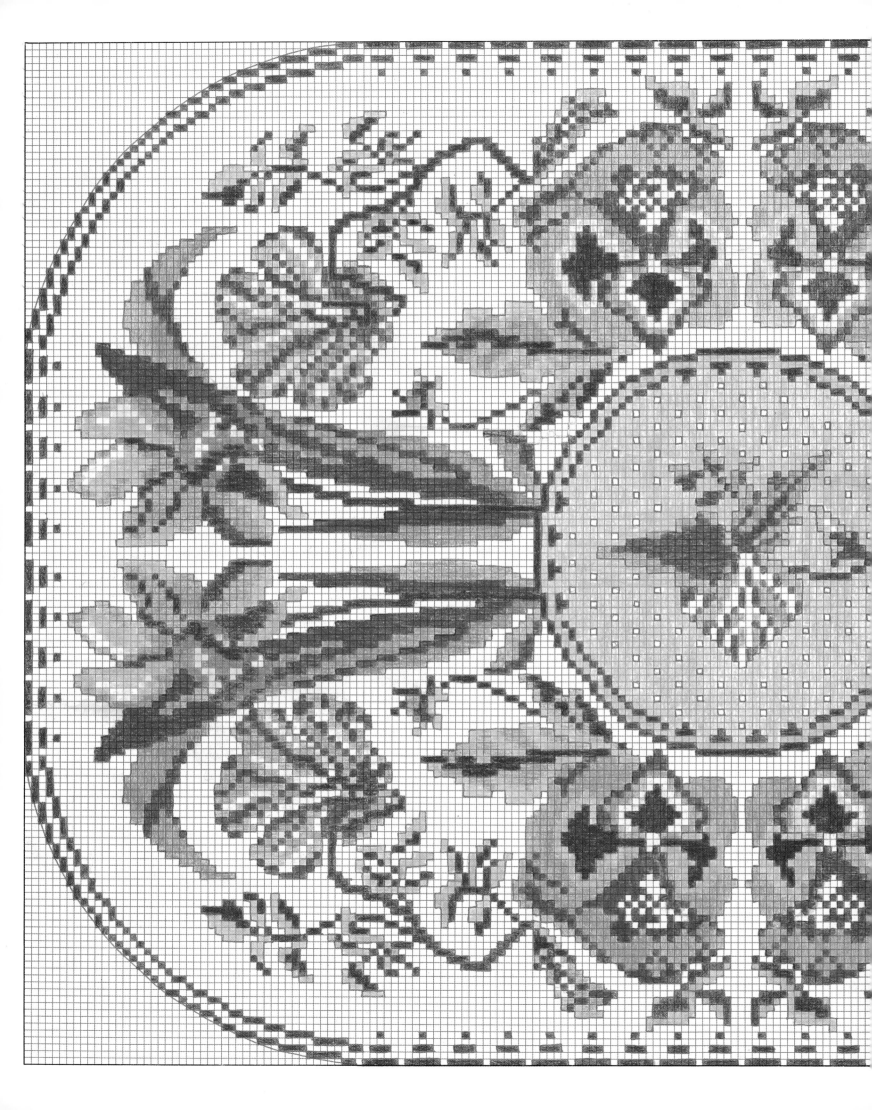

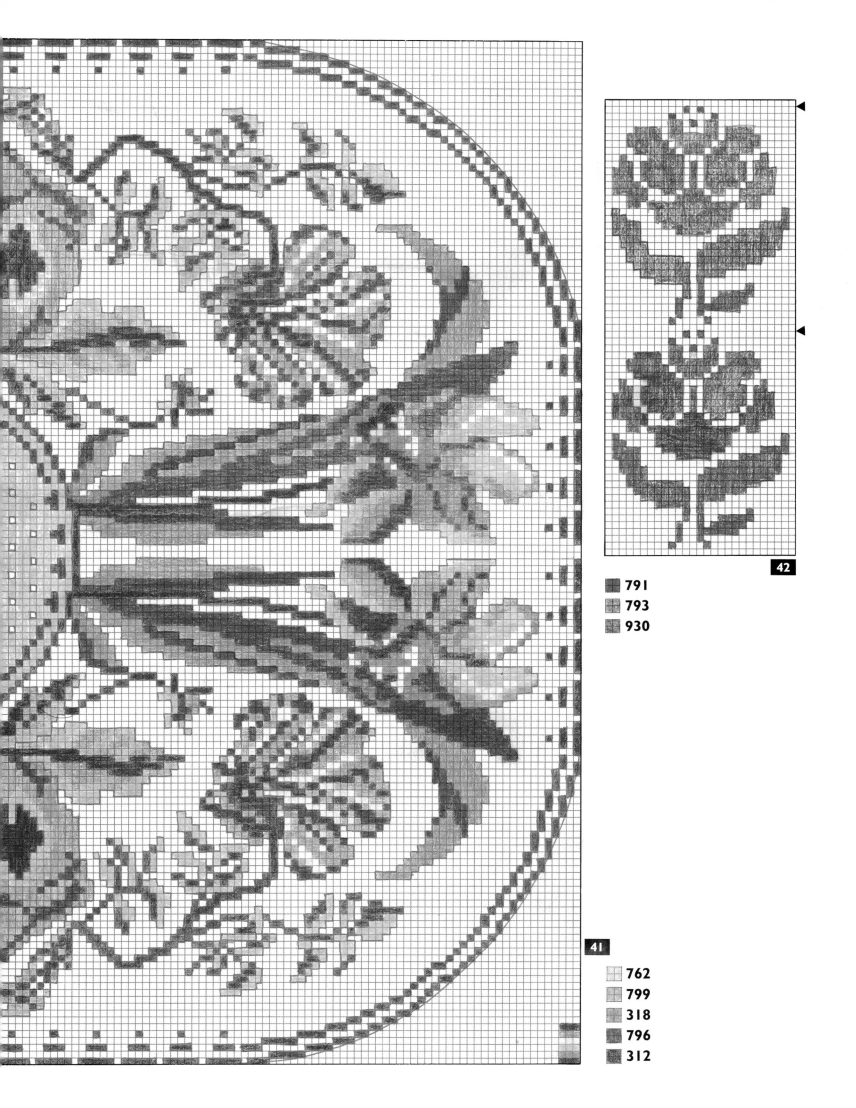

41

42

■ 791
▨ 793
▨ 930

▨ 762
▨ 799
▨ 318
■ 796
■ 312

Inspirations in
VIOLET

$\mathcal{T}$he blend of red and blue—opposites that attract—give life to the most tender lilac shades and the more striking purples.

Psychologists suggest that violet represents the inner self, the spirituality and the depth of feelings. According to religious tradition, it represents strength, mystery and passion. It is a colour of sensuality, power, pomp and luxury, and was the most renowned and valued colour in the old world. We will never know what that original colour's shading was, whether redder or bluer, because the murex, the mollusc from which the colour was first extracted, is extinct.

With the advent of synthetic dyes, all the shades of violet once again took centre stage. The French launched it into the fashion world with the name of mauve, and it did especially well in Victorian England. The colour violet was instrumental in bringing about another dye, called fuchsia after the flower. It was vibrant; a real cross between red and blue. A few days prior to the official launch, it was renamed magenta after the battle won by the French and the Piedmonts in 1859 against the Austrians.

The natural world is full of violet—in the mineral domain, amethyst sparkles in deep violet tones; in the floral domain, violet colours many flowers: wisteria, lavender, lilac, common mallow, fuchsia, pansies, iris and, of course, violet. This striking colour blooms readily in gardens, picturesque and artistic—Van Gogh painted dazzling scenes using violet.

The full cluster of our designs extol the sensuous vitality that makes violet both modern and captivating around the home.

Page 49: This garden corner is a copy of the real thing with the art of the painter reflected in the style of the embroidery. The fascinating shades of violet, backed up by the green of the leaves and the golden tones of the ground, brilliantly capture the style of the impressionist painter. This piece would make a wonderful wall panel, cushion, bag or screen. For a more delicate touch, use a lighter fabric; for a more striking tone, use a thicker fabric. On Aida cloth with 72 stitches per 10 cm, a single thread of stranded cotton is needed. For 55 stitches per 10 cm, use two threads.

Above: From the bulbs spring narrow buds, big leaves, and bursting corollas. The incredible velvety colour of the real flowers on the right is mirrored in the tone of both the painted and embroidered ones: as a runner or tablecloth, this makes a great coordinating item to give your decor both originality and cheerfulness.

Opposite: The motif of the iris is presented in a double row to give an outdoor look to a table runner or the band on a tablecloth; or, you can isolate a bud, as we have, for a matching touch on a napkin. You will need to precisely measure up the length of the fabric against the pattern to ensure that the finished embroidery is centred. This method of repeating a motif is adopted more and more frequently because it allows greater flexibility in the use of the design.

This delightful iris motif creates a striking border with the help of an Aida fabric band. The band can be obtained in a ready-to-use form and can be attached to sheets, tablecloths or towels. The design is adapted to fit the band. Notice in the detailed shot that space has been left above and below the band. This is to allow room for attaching the band to the selected item.

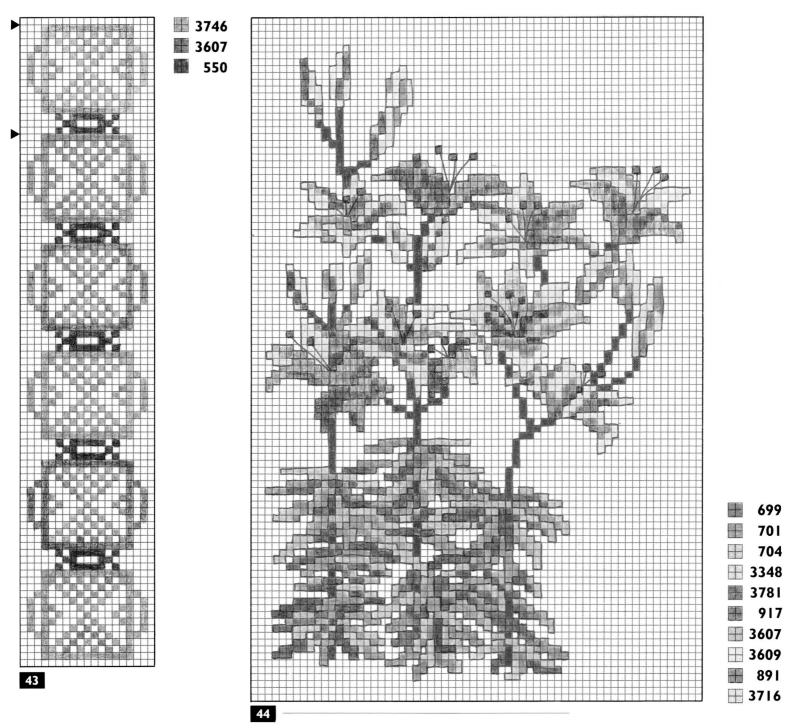

Inspirations in Violet

THE DESIGNS

43

	3746
	3607
	550

	699
	701
	704
	3348
	3781
	917
	3607
	3609
	891
	3716

44

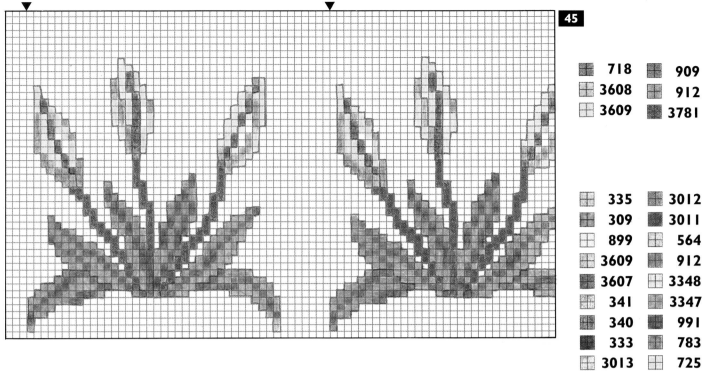

45

▦	718	▦	909
⊞	3608	⊞	912
⊞	3609	▦	3781

⊞	335	▦	3012
▦	309	▦	3011
⊞	899	⊞	564
▦	3609	▦	912
▦	3607	⊞	3348
▦	341	▦	3347
▦	340	▦	991
▦	333	▦	783
⊞	3013	⊞	725

47

⊞	743	▦	550
▦	721	▦	701
▦	554	▦	699
▦	917		

46

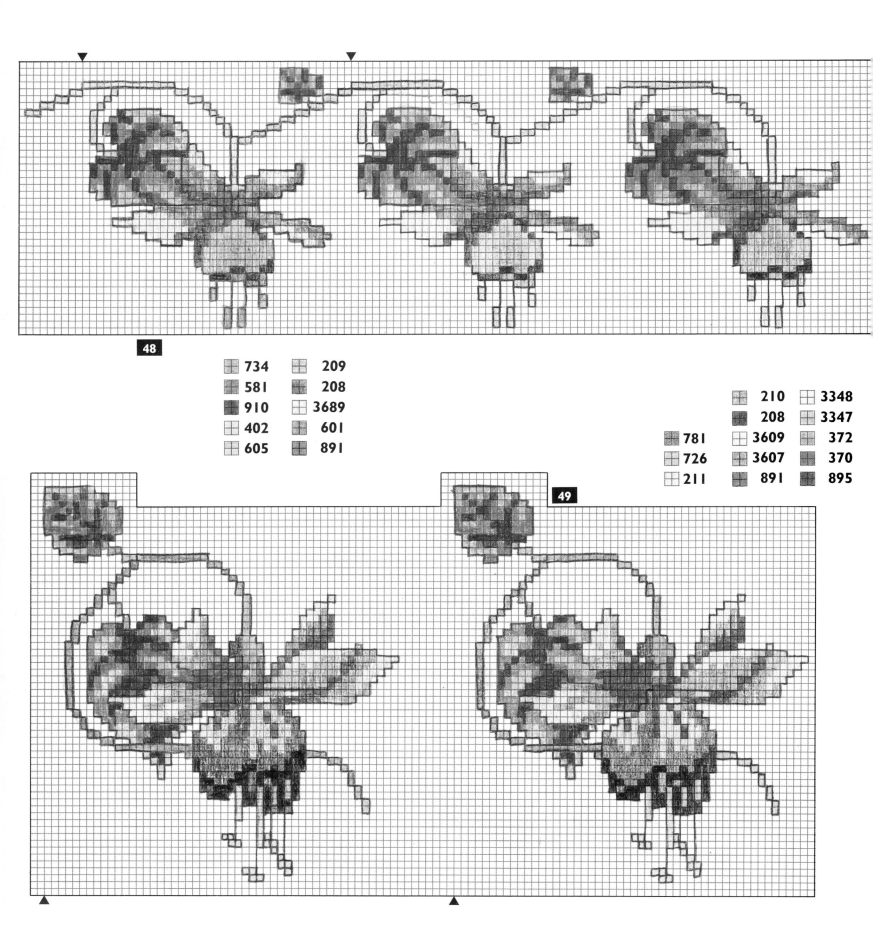

48

734		209	
581		208	
910		3689	
402		601	
605		891	

	210		3348
	208		3347
781	3609		372
726	3607		370
211	891		895

49

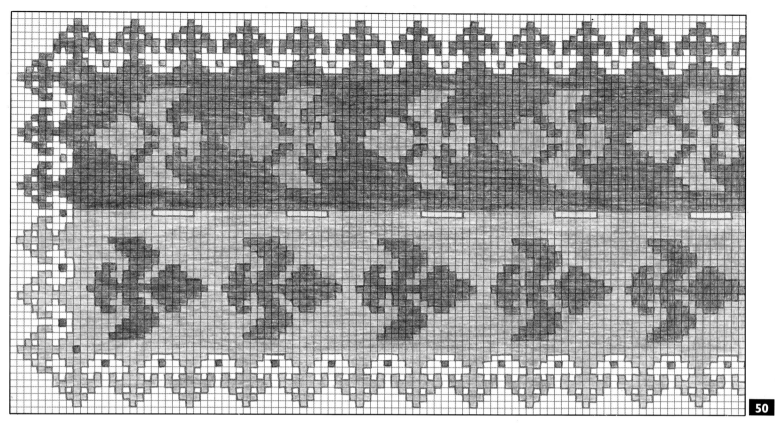

50

51

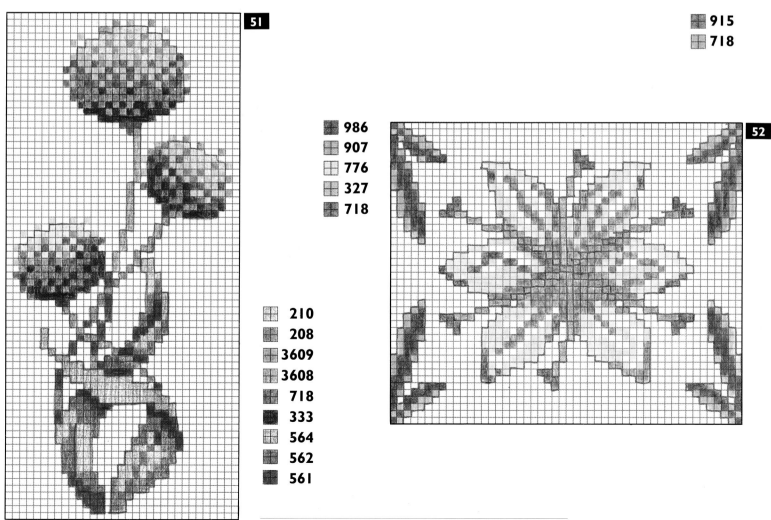

915
718

986
907
776
327
718

210
208
3609
3608
718
333
564
562
561

52

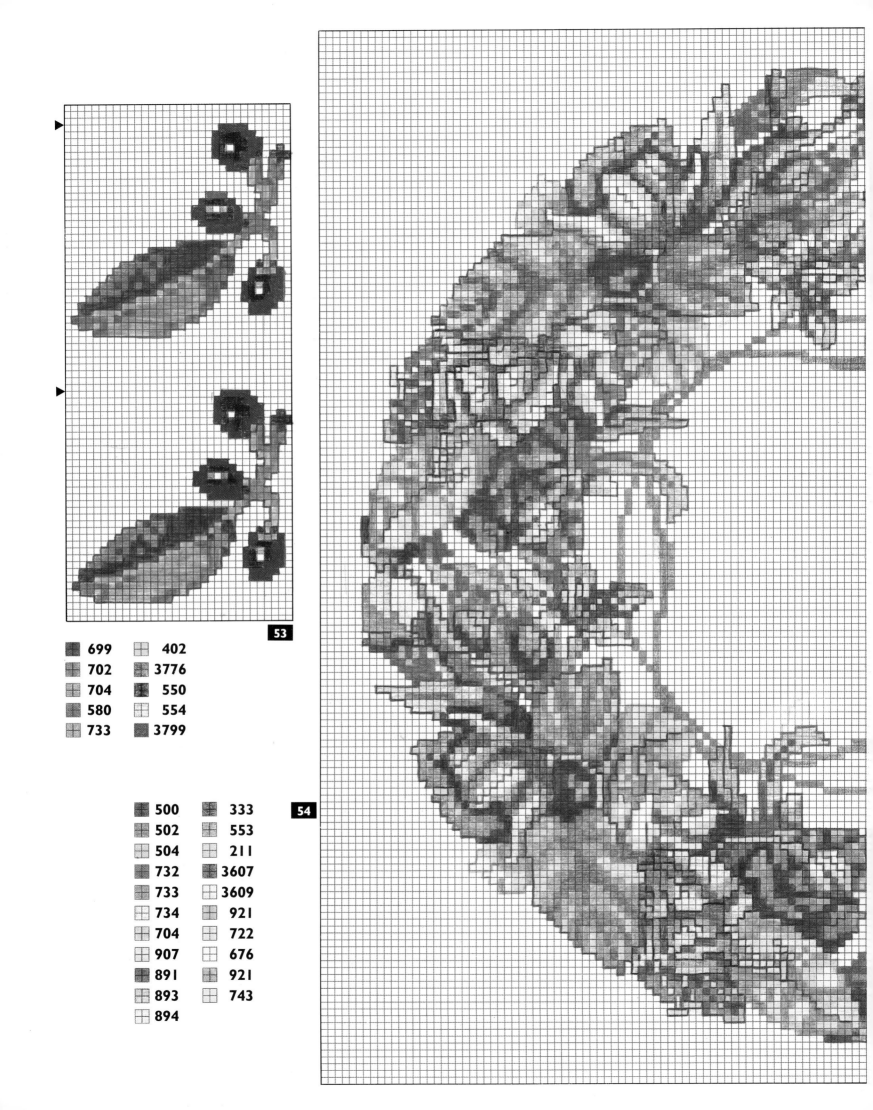

53

■	699	⊞	402
⊞	702	▦	3776
⊞	704	▨	550
■	580	⊞	554
⊞	733	▨	3799

54

▨	500	▨	333
⊞	502	⊞	553
⊞	504	⊞	211
▨	732	▦	3607
⊞	733	⊞	3609
⊞	734	⊞	921
⊞	704	⊞	722
⊞	907	⊞	676
▦	891	⊞	921
⊞	893	⊞	743
⊞	894		

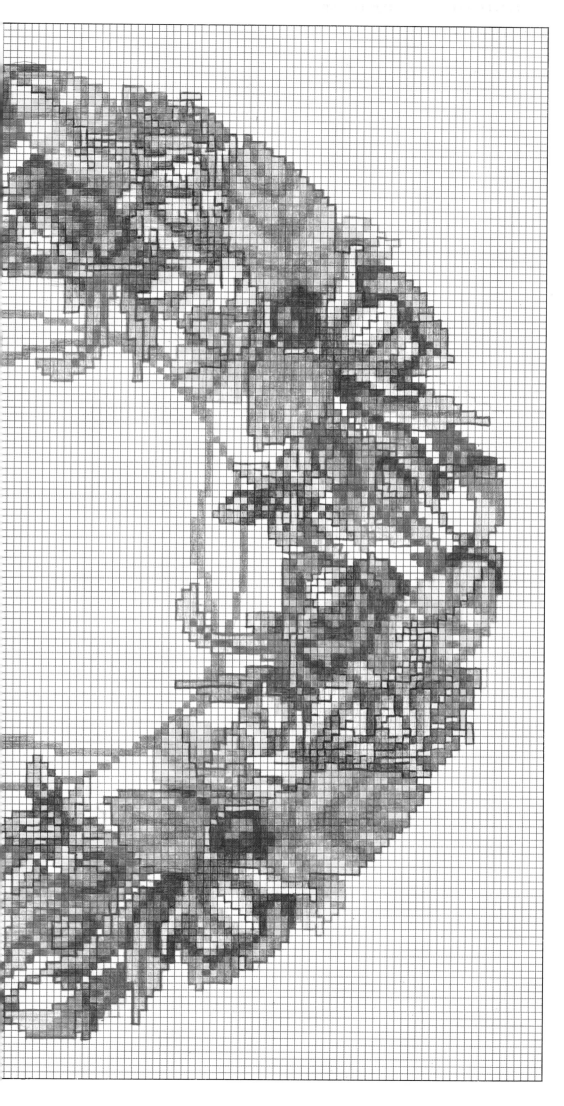
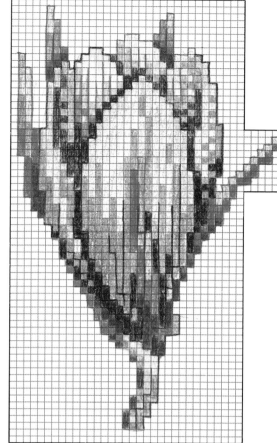

■	561	⊞	341
▦	909	▦	400
▦	910	▦	301
▦	955	▦	3776
■	333	⊞	402
▦	3746		
⊞	554		
▦	552		
■	550		

Inspirations in
YELLOW

*L*et yourself be inspired and captivated by the brilliance of yellow—it is beautiful; a colour full of sunshine. It looks wonderful on a table, and radiates from flowers like mimosas and jonquils. Yellow captures attention like the tang of a lemon or grapefruit. It harmonises with wood and takes on an old gold glow. In China it was the colour of the emperor, forbidden to all subjects. For Buddhists it represents the harmony of existence. It is the colour of light and as such it is joyful and triumphant.

It has brilliant clarity that can be shaded towards ochre, brown or green. It abounds in nature: saffron and banana, egg yolk and ripe wheat, buttercups and sunflowers, canary feathers and cat's eyes. It is also the colour of gold—the symbol of the earth's riches and the highest sign of glory, power and triumph.

In springtime gardens flourish with the yellow hues of daffodils, crocus, primroses and freesias. Even tender, new leaves have traces of yellow within their green. And, in the kitchen, it is a most appealing colour—the one that evokes savoury associations with the bounty of the table and the pleasure of food.

Yellow thread is a wonderful colour to embroider working in sunshine and cheerfulness, gathering life stitch by stitch.

𝒫age 60-61: The light of yellow thread glows against the white Aida as it forms a gentle zigzag of the narcissus. This effect is sunny and cheerful when worked along the drop of a tablecloth, on the side of an American sampler, on a sheet, on a small curtain, on a pinafore—or, in fact, anywhere. It is even possible to work out a corner design, using the mirror on the diagonal, or stopping the embroidery at the last flower and taking it up again on the other side. With corners use a small connecting motif such as a rhombus or a small star. (See p. 68)

𝓛eft and above: The ribbon and flower shoots create a playful and enchanting tablecloth. The ribbon wraps itself around a fine sequence of juniper berries in aerial spirals rich in gracefulness and shading. The pattern can also be repeated on the drop of the cloth. For decoration along the sides, try splitting the two motifs and alternating them in a balanced fashion within the empty spaces. Remember to mark the spots for the motifs at the beginning by tacking to achieve even spacing. (See p. 69)

*A*bove: A close-up section of the very fresh looking sampler on the right allows us to see and fully appreciate the shadings and tones. It also enables the easy counting of the cross stiches to accurately recreate a clear graph for a perfect result.

*R*ight: The full flavour of summer with baskets full of peaches and ripe pears, letters intertwined with juniper berries, and coloured bonsai. This sampler could be framed as a decoration for a wall, or the individual elements could be lifted out to become motifs for larger works. Begin the embroidery at the top left-hand corner and proceed diagonally towards the bottom right. (See pp. 72–73)

*L*eft: Fruit features once more in rows and groups and in wicker baskets: grapes, figs, oranges, bananas and cherries. All appear more lifelike due to the rich shading. This design can be used as a panel for the pages of a calendar or the weekly planner for meals. This planner would be perfect hanging in the kitchen mounted on a rectangular plywood frame that could even be lightly padded.

*T*his page: A closer look at the woven baskets shows how each one is different from the other. They are playfully worked to create the effect of different types of straw. Each basket also holds different fruits in natural colours. The fruit baskets can be copied without difficulty and reproduced in the centre of a tablecloth or at the bottom of a curtain where they will provide a new lift with a cheerful accent.

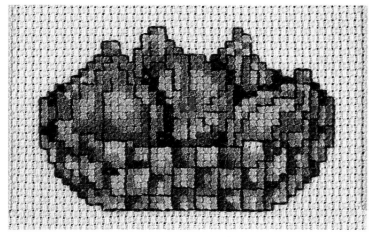

THE DESIGNS

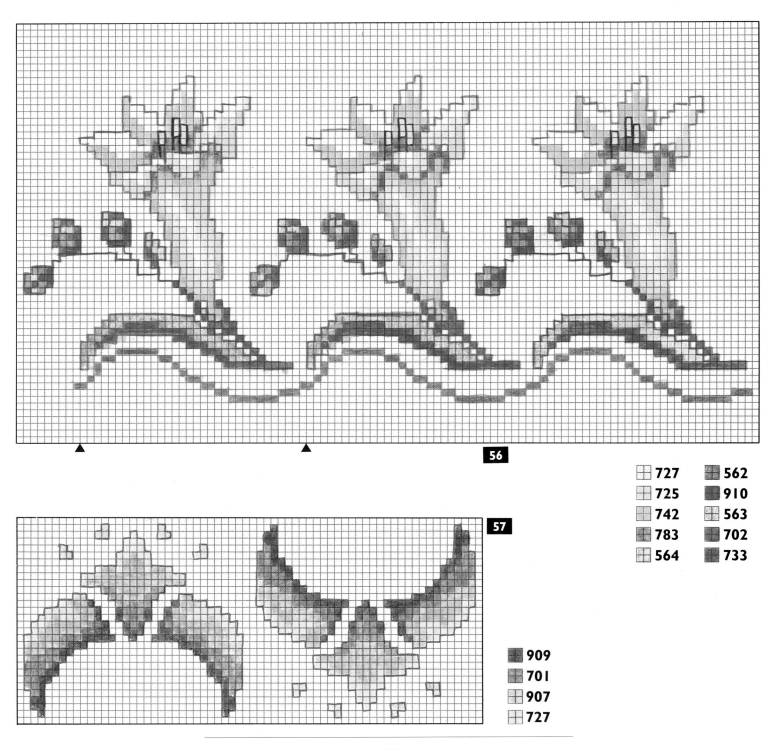

⊞ 727		▨ 562	
⊞ 725		■ 910	
⊞ 742		⊞ 563	
▨ 783		▨ 702	
⊞ 564		▨ 733	

■ 909	
▨ 701	
⊞ 907	
⊞ 727	

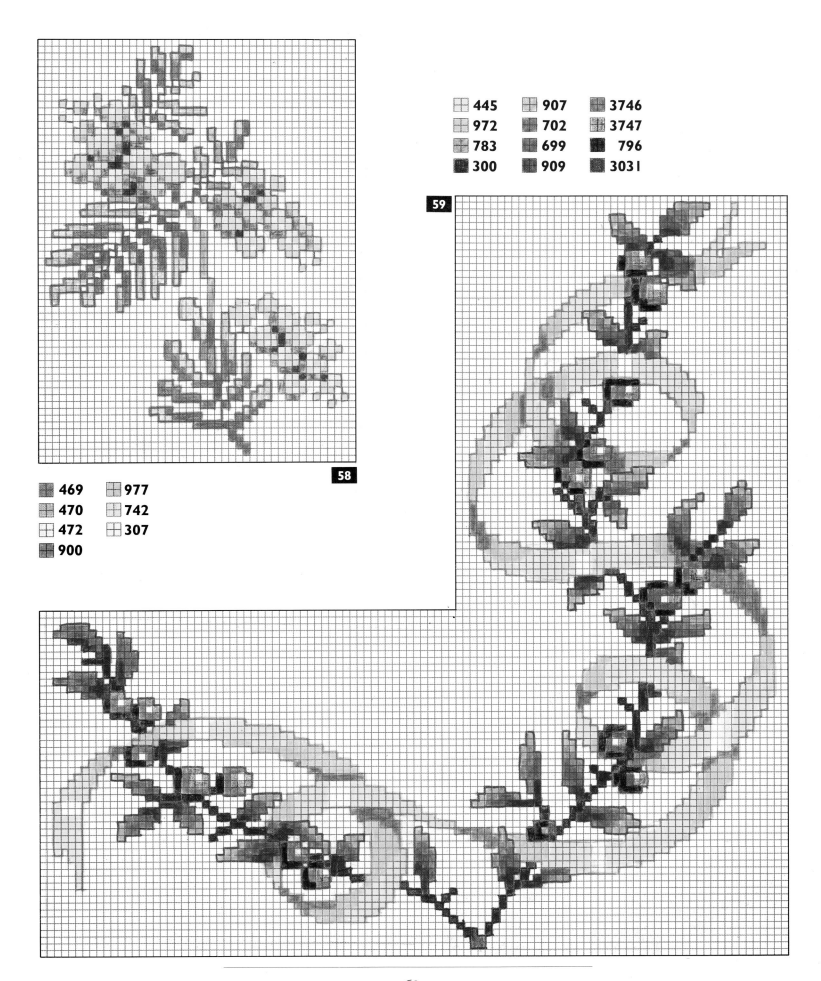

445   907   3746
972   702   3747
783   699   796
300   909   3031

469   977
470   742
472   307
900

58

59

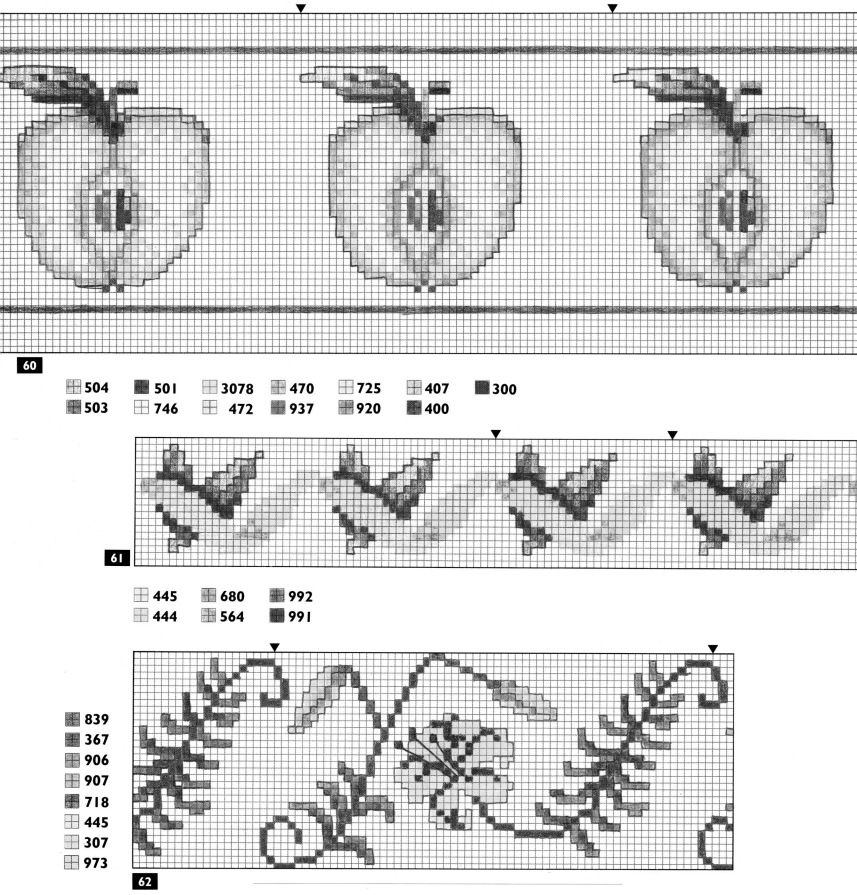

60

▦ 504	■ 501	▦ 3078	▦ 470	▦ 725	▦ 407	■ 300
▦ 503	▦ 746	▦ 472	▦ 937	▦ 920	▦ 400	

61

▦ 445	▦ 680	▦ 992
▦ 444	▦ 564	■ 991

▦ 839
▦ 367
▦ 906
▦ 907
▦ 718
▦ 445
▦ 307
▦ 973

62

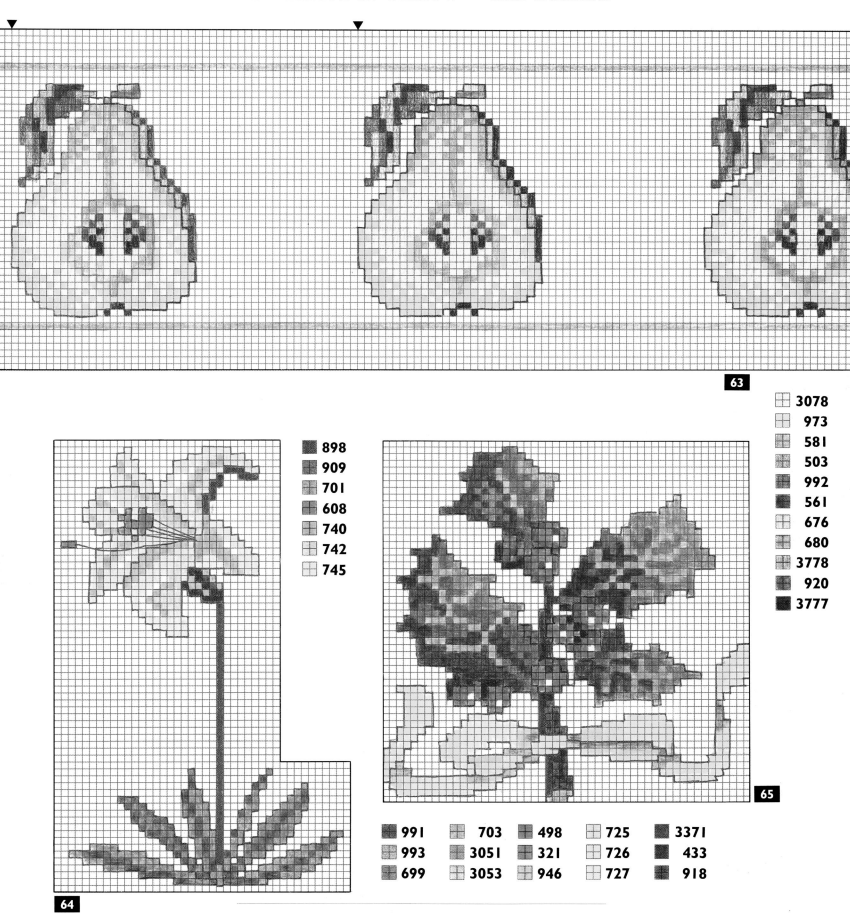

63

3078	
973	
581	
503	
992	
561	
676	
680	
3778	
920	
3777	

898	
909	
701	
608	
740	
742	
745	

64

65

991	703	498	725	3371
993	3051	321	726	433
699	3053	946	727	918

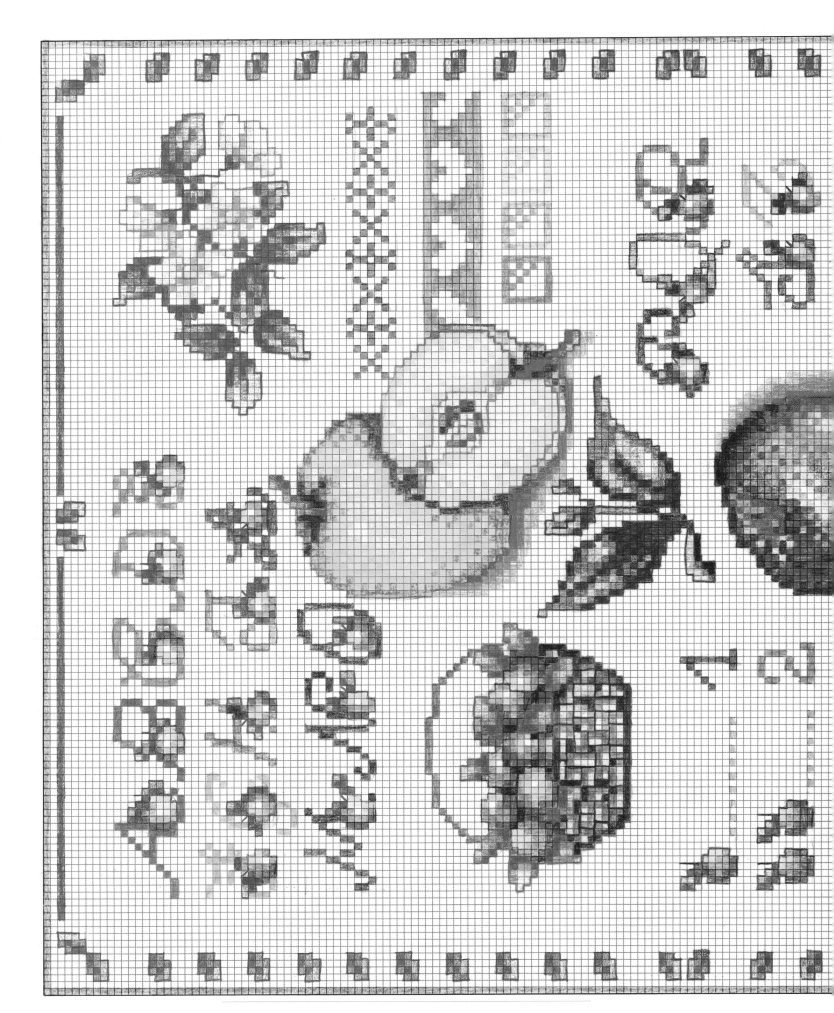

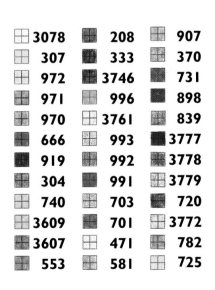

⊞ 3078	▦ 208	⊞ 907
⊞ 307	▦ 333	⊞ 370
⊞ 972	▦ 3746	▦ 731
▦ 971	▢ 996	▦ 898
⊞ 970	⊞ 3761	▦ 839
▦ 666	⊞ 993	■ 3777
■ 919	⊞ 992	▦ 3778
▦ 304	▦ 991	⊞ 3779
⊞ 740	⊞ 703	▦ 720
⊞ 3609	▦ 701	⊞ 3772
▦ 3607	⊞ 471	▦ 782
▦ 553	⊞ 581	⊞ 725

Inspirations in
ORANGE

Created by blending red and yellow, orange dazzles in its many shades. For centuries it had no real identity of its own and had to yield to the stronger impact of red. Fire flames and auburn hair, for example, both have chromatic tones that are, strictly speaking, part of the colour orange but have traditionally been defined as red. A few centuries ago the citrus fruit, aurantium, arrived in Europe from the East. Its decisive colouring and its exquisite, succulent pulp made a strong impression and the fruit was given the name, orange.

From a psychological viewpoint, orange remains closer to yellow than red—cheerful, expansive, extroverted, sun-filled. In the garden, autumn is orange's season as the leaves become golden and tawny. Other fruits with orange pulp are the mango, the persimmon, and the apricot which resembles watered silk. In the vegetable domain orange is found in the familiar carrot, squash and pumpkin. A darker tone is found in certain exotic spices such as the intoxicating cinnamon. An earthy shade like no other, orange is found in the iron deposits that tinge many rocks including amber, quartz and carnelian, and in certain types of wood that are tawny rather than white.

The flames of a fireplace also reflect a brown-orange light tone that warms up surrounding terracotta and bricks. For this reason alone, orange cannot be omitted from embroidery threads because it represents a sense of home and welcome: the warmth from the chimney, the glow from the hearth, symbolic and central to the meaning of family.

Pages 74–76: Spots of warming light with explosions of rich colour tones highlight rustic beauty in the centre of a tablecloth. With a square tablecloth, the motifs should be equidistant from each other. With a rectangular cloth, the long sides can be inter-spersed with small clusters of fruit and leaves which can also be featured on the drop of the tablecloth and on napkins. Thanks to cross stitch, the ribbon has all the richness of a strip of satin, and the blue flowers set-off the ripening fruit. (See p. 84)

Right: Here we have fruits of the forest surrounded by green, then finished with rich strokes of sunny tones. Only a few leaves and a simple vine shoot are needed to create a colourful splash on a tablecloth, towel, curtain, or sheet. Repeating the motif on the fabric is very effective and results in a rich border.

*L*eft: A branch of wood, a shoot of vine leaves and a cluster of juniper berries on this fabric kindle the desire to be surrounded by natural colours. The design unfolds in zigzag fashion on a strip measuring 70 stitches in length. Whether the branch finishes on the right or the left, the motif can be repeated as often as desired. (See p. 87)

*A*bove: Orange hues suit this design admirably. The playful leaves lend excitement to the napkin, which is no bigger than 42 stitches in length. This pattern gives the table an unusual charm. Before beginning the embroidery, carefully plan the motifs in order to explore the numerous adaptations possible with regards to the desired look of the finished product. To decorate the corners, embroider two branches, joining them with a small sprinkling of leaves.

*L*eft: Delicious looking, minature fruits are quick to work in cross stitch. Embroidered with two threads, these topiary-like fruit trees make a delightfully different combination. A panel decorated with lots of little trees would create a stunning headboard for a bed. Cushions and other soft furnishings can be decorated with small trees of two different sizes. The possibilities are appealing, simple and endless. (See p. 86)

*A*bove: Simplicity, beauty and colour are the three best qualities of cross stitch. This basic design illustrates how a simple tablecloth can be transformed into a showpiece with the repetition of a motif along the border—the end result is a colourful latticework design. The shape of the tablecloth is not important, as the design can be spaced to suit. (See p. 85)

Inspirations in Orange
THE DESIGNS

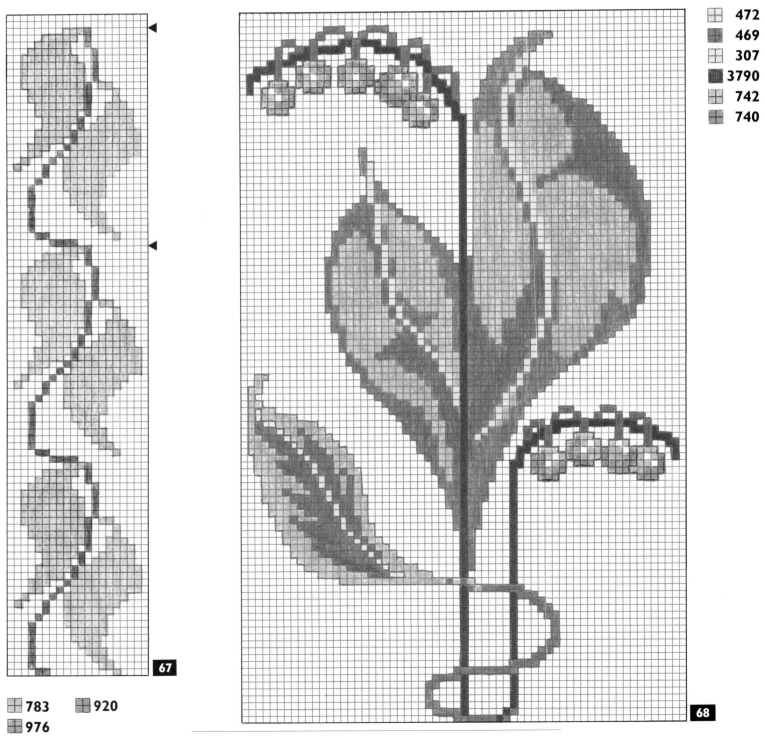

▦	472
▦	469
▦	307
▦	3790
▦	742
▦	740

67

68

▦	783	▦	920
▦	976		

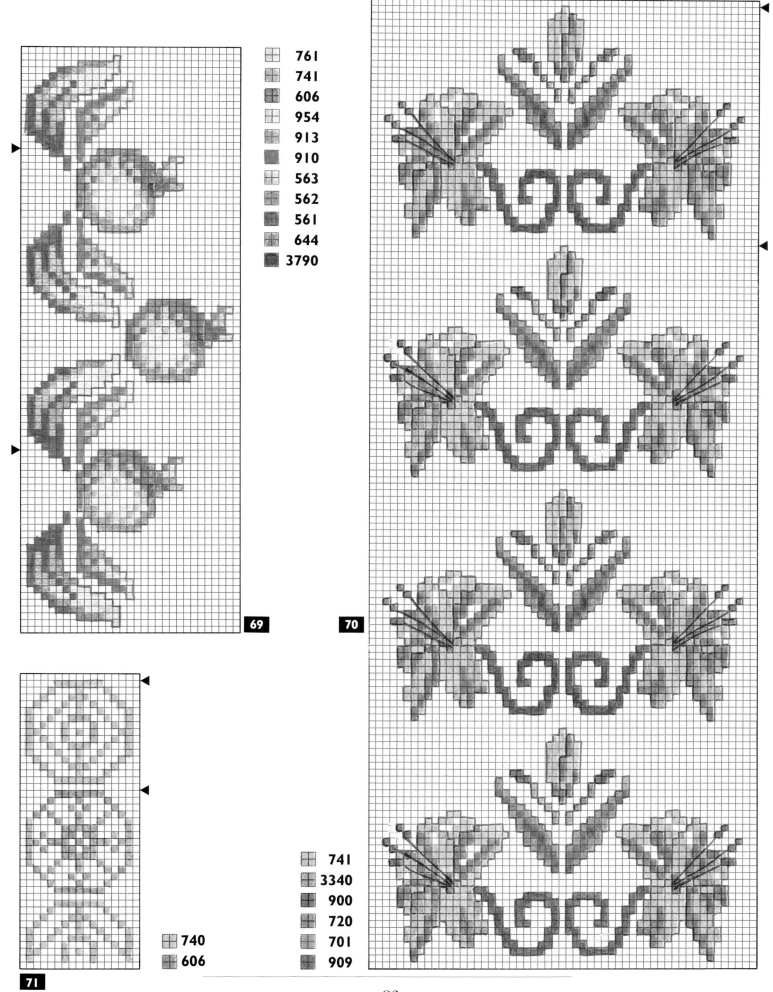

761
741
606
954
913
910
563
562
561
644
3790

69

70

740
606

71

741
3340
900
720
701
909

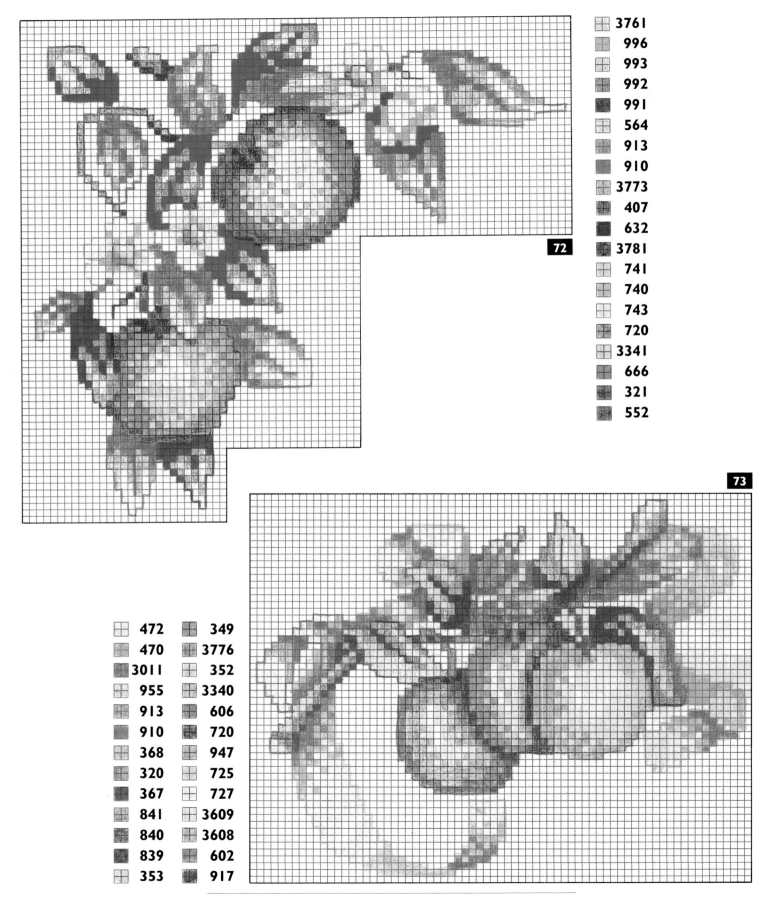

3761
996
993
992
991
564
913
910
3773
407
632

72

3781
741
740
743
720
3341
666
321
552

73

472		349	
470		3776	
3011		352	
955		3340	
913		606	
910		720	
368		947	
320		725	
367		727	
841		3609	
840		3608	
839		602	
353		917	

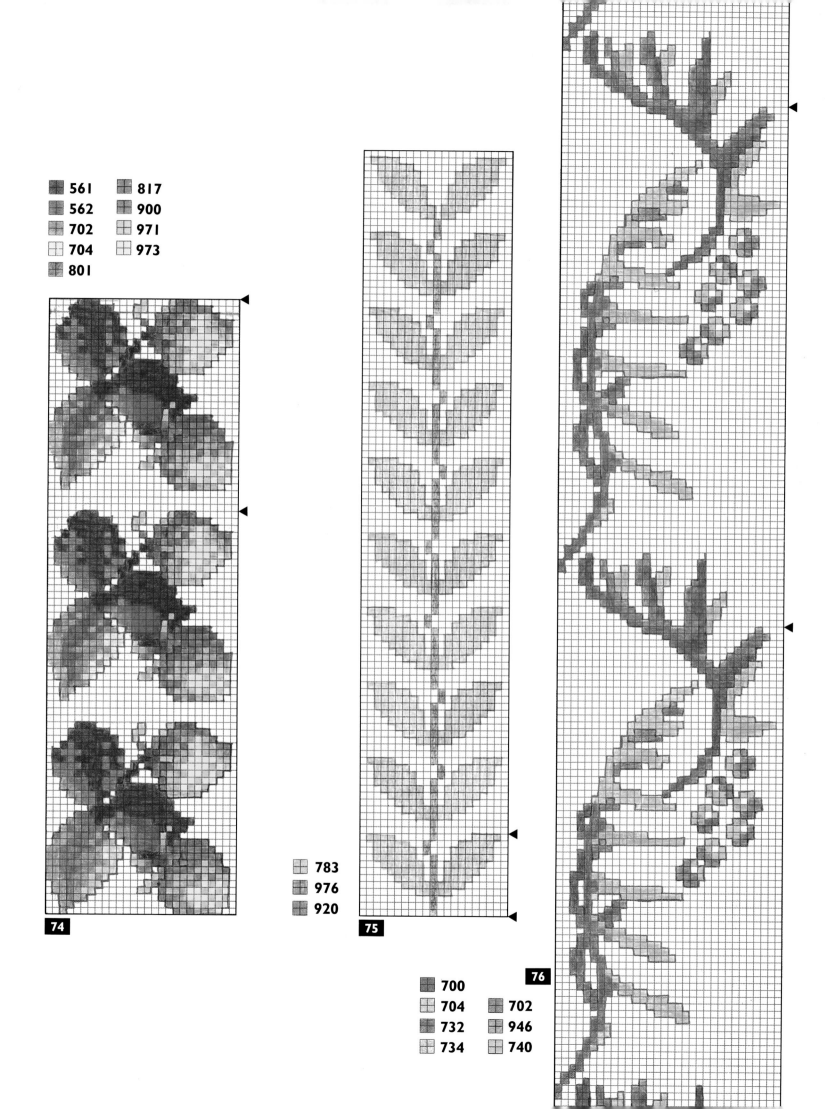

561   817
562   900
702   971
704   973
801

74

783
976
920

75

700
704   702
732   946
734   740

76

77

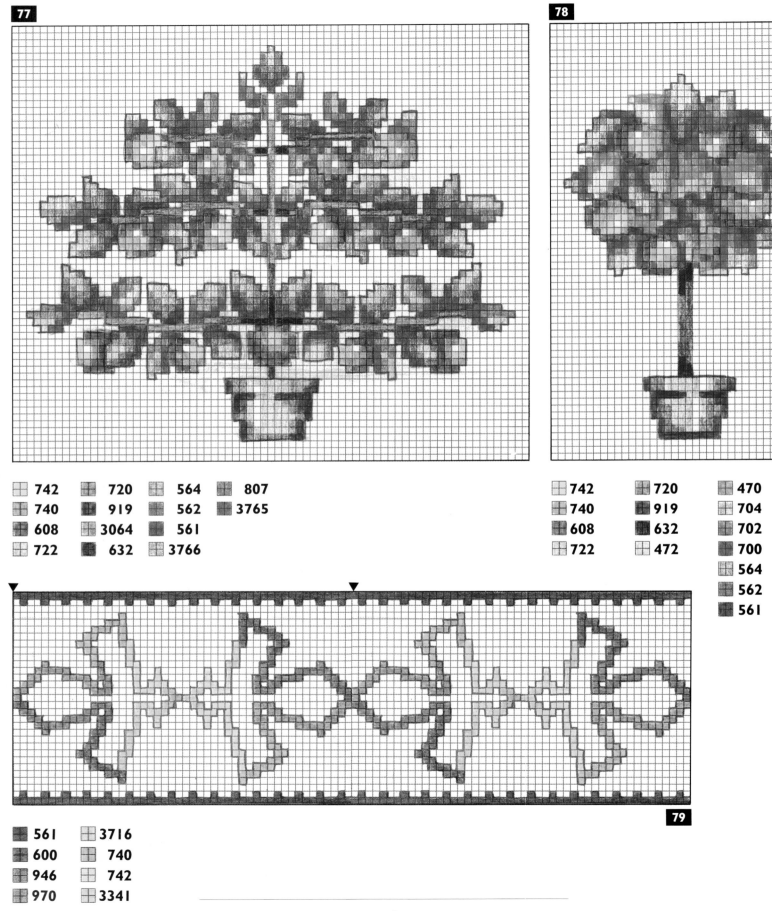

78

742	720	564	807			
740	919	562	3765			
608	3064	561				
722	632	3766				

742	720	470
740	919	704
608	632	702
722	472	700
		564
		562
		561

79

561	3716
600	740
946	742
970	3341

81

▦	3341
▦	350
▦	817
▦	975
▦	977
▦	731
▦	472
▦	702
▦	700
▦	699

80

▦	3779	▦	919
▦	722	▦	504
▦	720	▦	502

Inspirations in
RED

$\mathscr{S}$top! Attention! Danger! Red also indicates courage, daring and dynamism. Red is the colour of the blood that pulses in our veins and the heart that beats in our breast. It expresses the strongest of emotions and the most intense feelings and sensations. The attributes of red are nearly always superlatives. It is at the top of the rainbow. It is the first tone to strike the conscious self when we wake up. More than any other colour it attracts the eye, mesmerises, gives weight, touches the soul and unleashes anger and rage.

Passion is red, as are the pleasures of the senses. It is sumptuous, rich and regal, flashy, symbolic, spectacular—hence the colour of the stage curtain and of the carpet we roll out to welcome dignitaries and heroes. It is the colour that best expresses the joy and excitement of festivals like Christmas—the cheerfulness of the juniper berries amidst the green holly, apples amongst the spruce branches, ribbons and bows on presents under the sparkling tree. It is the sharp, tempting colour of fruits which are irresistible—cherries, strawberries, raspberries and red currants. It is also the hot flavour of that most sublime fruit, the spicy red chilli pepper.

In embroidery red has always had a very secure place. In the last century it was the colour used for the numbers or initials on personal linen. Its deep tones denote richness and its lighter tones youth and vivaciousness. Red thread has the capacity to enrich a fabric and highlight any designs.

𝒫age 88 and 89: The border pattern of cherries create a striking effect on an old sideboard cabinet. Larger motifs would look great on a carpet. Alternatively, a single cherry could be embroidered onto a very fine fabric such as pure linen and made into a brooch using a double thickness of thread. (See p. 98)

ℒeft: The red of the juniper berry contrasts with the green shade of the leaves. This fresh, innocent design, never tedious or unappealing, is often used in the embroidery tradition of cross stitch. It is popular, no doubt, because of the beauty of line, the cheerful colours, and for its appeal as a decoration. A helpful hint: do a quick sketch of the design, in colour and drawn to scale, to gauge an idea of the finished piece before beginning cross stitching. (See p. 96)

𝒜bove: A bouquet, a ribbon and lots of complementary colours give this piece of embroidery style and class. This design would be ideal for a cushion, a linen bag, or a handkerchief. (See p. 99)

*A*bove and right: A garland creates a festive season on a tablecloth, a tray, or a cushion. Take care to centre the motif by planning the exact position. Count the stitches both vertically and horizontally to make a square and trace the diagonals. Do the same on the fabric and start embroidering on the vertical point in the centre. (See pp. 100–101)

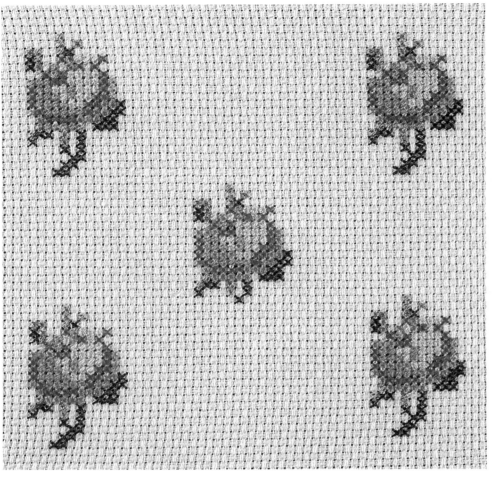

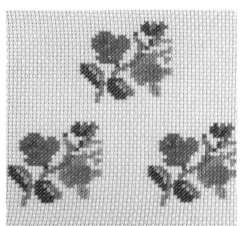

*A*bove and right: These little, graceful and unique touches of light create a charming design for a table-cloth. Using all the different variations, the very striking effect will resemble a classical damask of fine silk from the 1800s. This piece illustrates perfectly the subtle fascination of an easy stitch that never varies its geometric repetition, yet can be transformed and enhanced with colour and design.

Inspirations in Red
THE DESIGNS

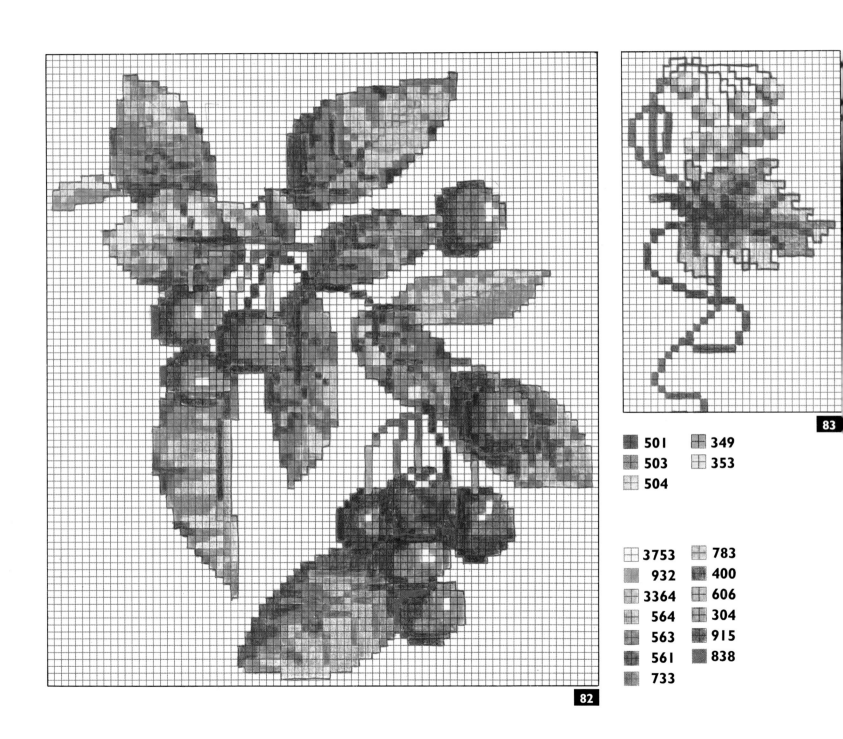

■ 501	⊞ 349	
⊞ 503	⊞ 353	
⊞ 504		

⊞ 3753	⊞ 783	
932	■ 400	
⊞ 3364	⊞ 606	
⊞ 564	⊞ 304	
⊞ 563	■ 915	
⊞ 561	■ 838	
■ 733		

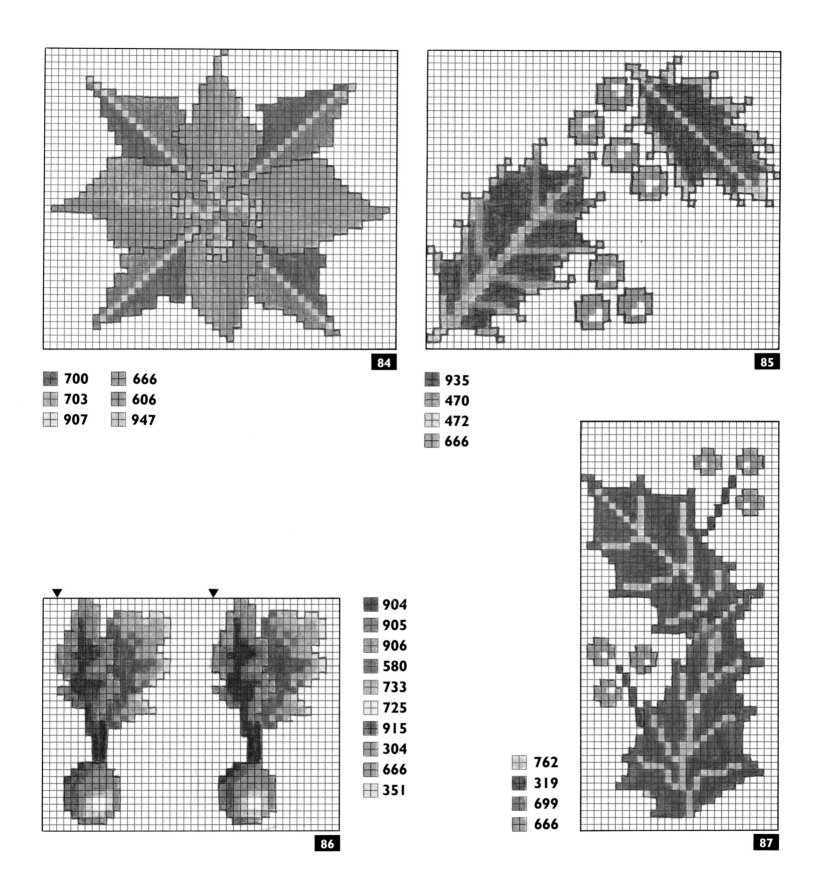

84

■ 700 ▦ 666
▦ 703 ▦ 606
▦ 907 ▦ 947

85

■ 935
▦ 470
▦ 472
▦ 666

■ 904
▦ 905
▦ 906
■ 580
▦ 733
▦ 725
▦ 915
▦ 304
▦ 666
▦ 351

86

▦ 762
■ 319
■ 699
▦ 666

87

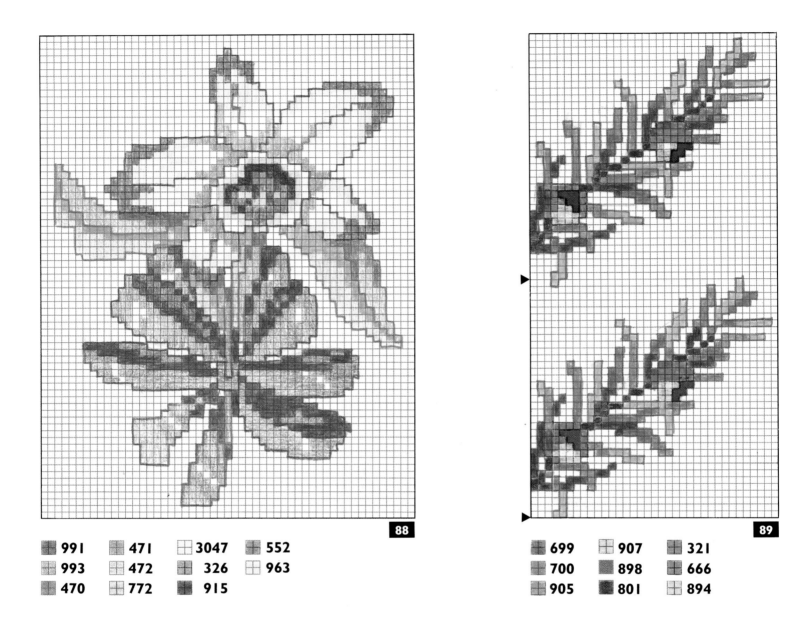

88

▨ 991	▨ 471	⊞ 3047	▨ 552
▨ 993	⊞ 472	▨ 326	⊞ 963
▨ 470	⊞ 772	▨ 915	

89

▨ 699	⊞ 907	▨ 321
▨ 700	▨ 898	▨ 666
▨ 905	▨ 801	⊞ 894

90

▨	699
▨	701
▨	703
▨	433
▨	600
▨	666
▨	917
⊞	754

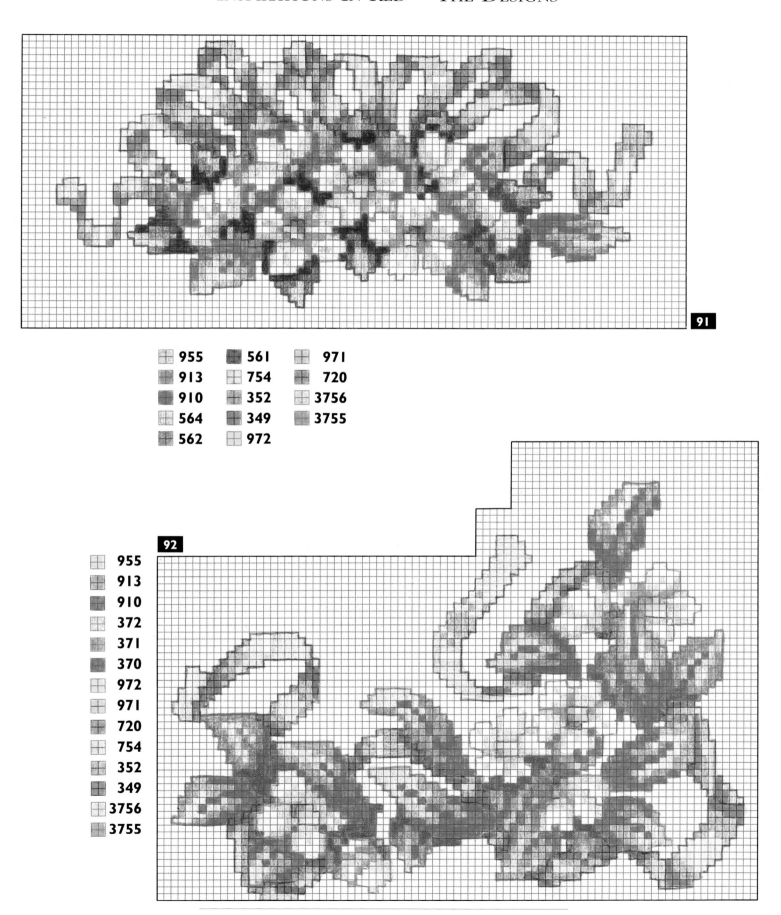

91

⊞	955	▦	561	⊞	971
▦	913	⊞	754	▦	720
▦	910	▦	352	▦	3756
⊞	564	▦	349	▦	3755
⊞	562	⊞	972		

92

⊞	955
▦	913
▦	910
⊞	372
▦	371
▦	370
⊞	972
⊞	971
▦	720
⊞	754
▦	352
▦	349
⊞	3756
▦	3755

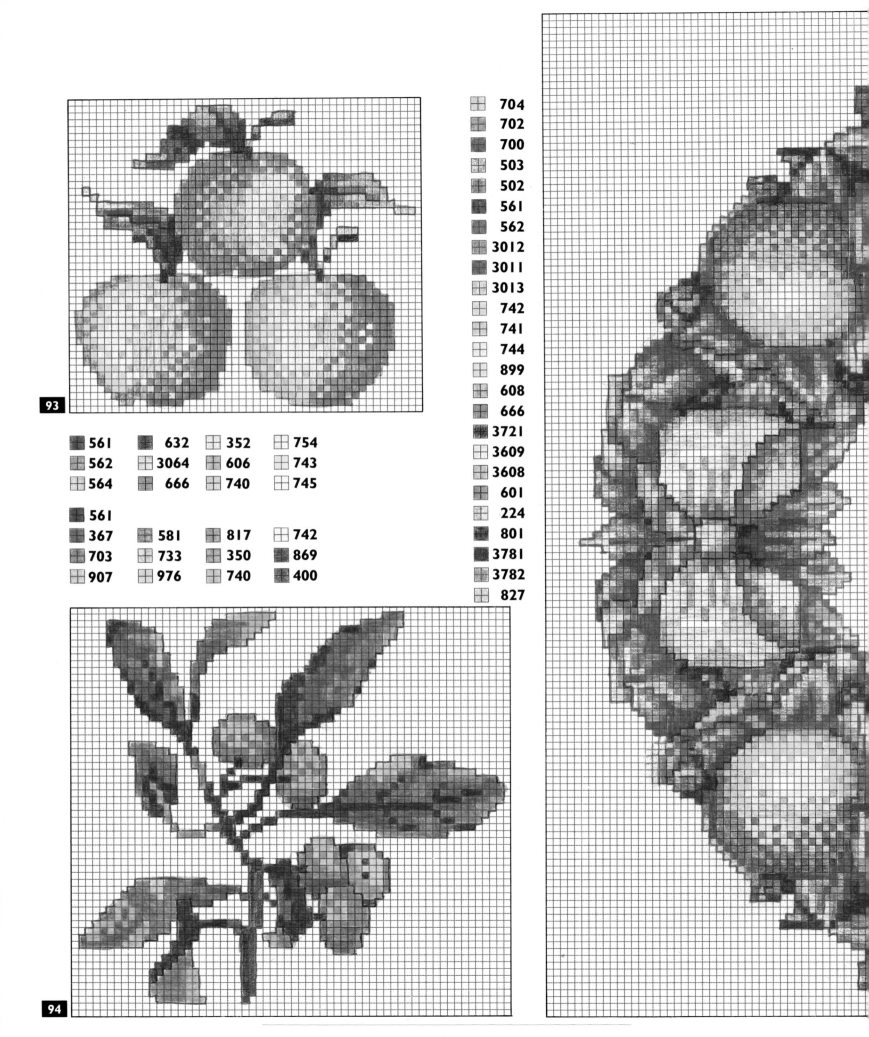

561 632 352 754
562 3064 606 743
564 666 740 745

561
367 581 817 742
703 733 350 869
907 976 740 400

704
702
700
503
502
561
562
3012
3011
3013
742
741
744
899
608
666
3721
3609
3608
601
224
801
3781
3782
827

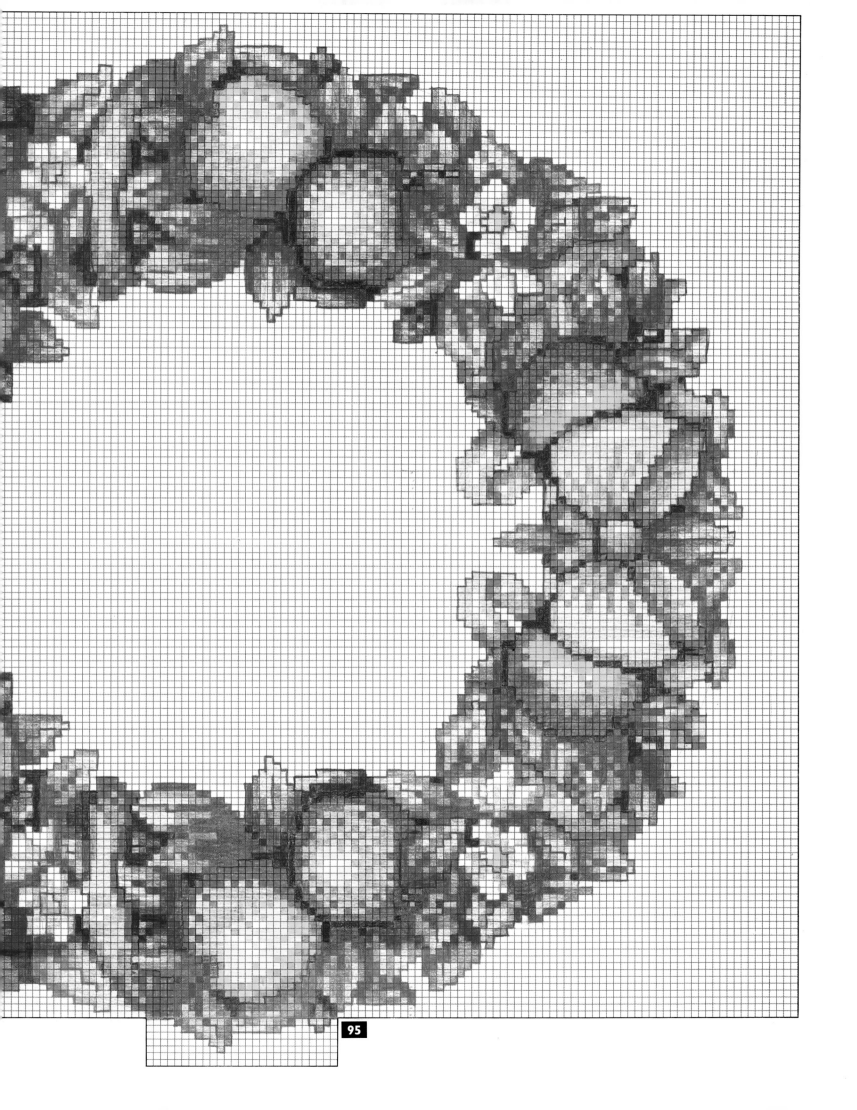

Inspirations in GREEN

*G*reen, in embroidery, is often the colour that complements or provides background. Leafy branches, foliage and grass always make a good frame in soft shades of green or stronger and more pronounced tones. This is because green highlights the red of a juniper berry, the rose of petals and the yellow and orange of fruit and vegetables. The effect created is that of a totally natural, eye pleasing and reassuring contrast.

But green also makes a great dominant colour that is calming, peaceful and restful. The more vibrant shades of green provide a clarity that represents rebirth in springtime and reflects the hope and renewal of that season.

Even though vegetation is abundantly represented through the richness of green, nature has, at the same time, skilfully protected itself from too much interference from human endeavour. There are, for example, few green mineral substances from which pigments and dye can be obtained. The discovery of the shade known as 'green jade of Scotland' is a rare exception. It was discovered centuries ago in a stone and was hailed as a milestone in dye-making research.

This wonderfully natural colour surrounds us in grass and the leafy branches of trees and provides its own fascinating world of fantasy—dragons, monsters, elves and alien creatures are often represented in green. There is a similar magic in the 'green ray' that sometimes appears in the sky before the sun sets on the day.

Few of us realise that green is also the colour of the planet Venus, and in certain countries, by association, it was customary to dress in green for weddings as Venus symbolised love.

*P*ages 102–103: Here are three borders reminiscent of the geometric folk designs of Greece, Russia and the Great North. The folkloric designs often feature yellow and red, but in the three borders presented, green mixed with white predominates to provide a striking decorative effect. The borders, carefully positioned, can decorate a table napkin, a cushion or a curtain. Begin the embroidery at one side, working on all three borders as you move between the edges of the frame. On the left, the close-up detail of the design shows that while it may appear complicated, it is, in fact, quite straight-forward and simple whether worked horizontally or vertically.

𝒜bove and right: A delightful, miniature garden adds life to a set of towels. The gracefulness of the tiny flowers with the gentle touch of green creates the delicate effect of Liberty lines in the design. The design is beautiful as a main feature but can also be worked as a border using the same colours but altering the shades of each mini-bouquet. This shading is very eye-catching on a curtain, quilt, or tablecloth. On the edge of a towel in Aida fabric, which allows 50 stitches every 10 cm, the motif is approximately 5 cm in height. If you choose Aida fabric of 44 or 55 stitches every 10 cm, the same design will be roughly 6 or 4 cm in height respectively.

Above: Garlands can offer many variations. The designs can complete a gift, a placemat or a box. The two garlands linked here with a pink ribbon can decorate a curtain or an American sampler. The motif can also be used as a border. It will, however, be a fairly large border as each garland requires 46 stitches. The size of the garland can be increased if, instead of working on every bundle of the fabric edge, each cross stitch is embroidered over two bundles, remembering to double the thread. (See p. 112)

Right: The yellow juniper berry evokes an impression of summer; red of Christmas. For a look that is very refined, try colouring berries blue or lilac and the leaves and branches in a darker shade. (See pp. 110 and 113)

THE DESIGNS

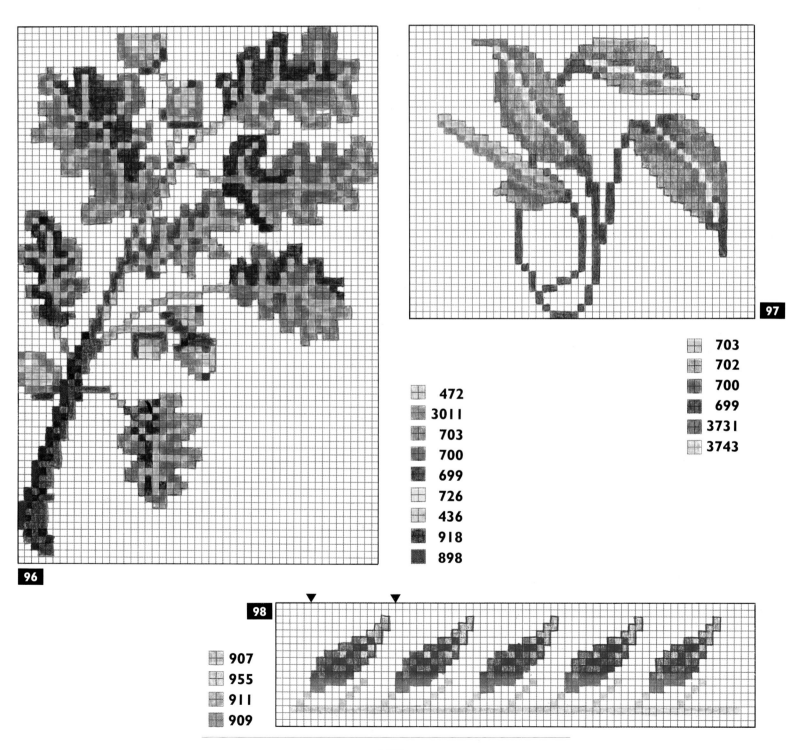

96

472
3011
703
700
699
726
436
918
898

97

703
702
700
699
3731
3743

98

907
955
911
909

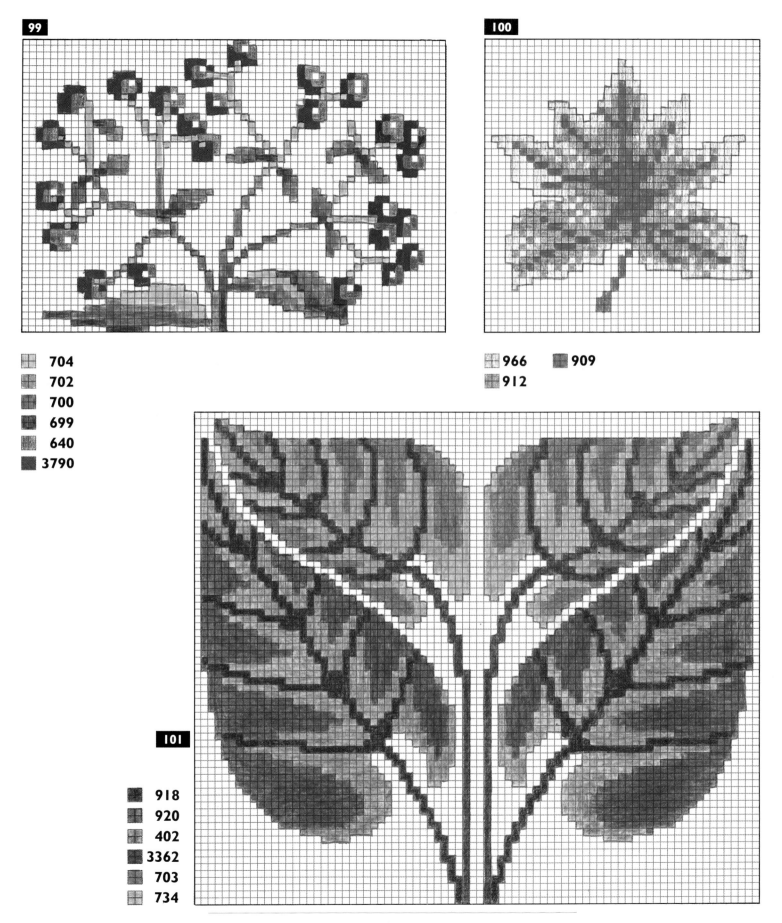

99

100

101

704
702
700
699
640
3790

966   909
912

918
920
402
3362
703
734

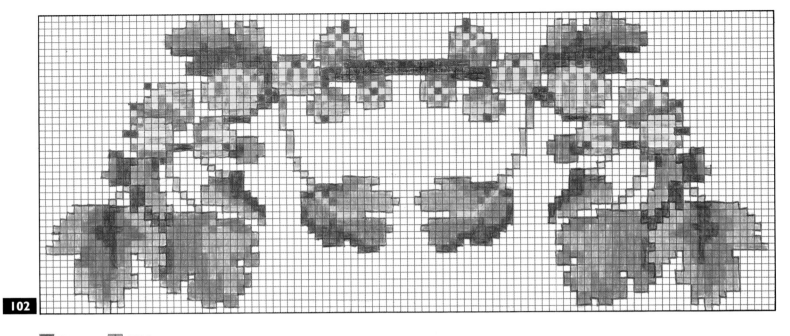

102

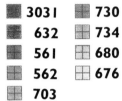

■	3031	■	730
■	632	⊞	734
■	561	⊞	680
■	562	⊞	676
⊞	703		

⊞	904
■	905
⊞	907
■	580
⊞	734
⊞	3753

103

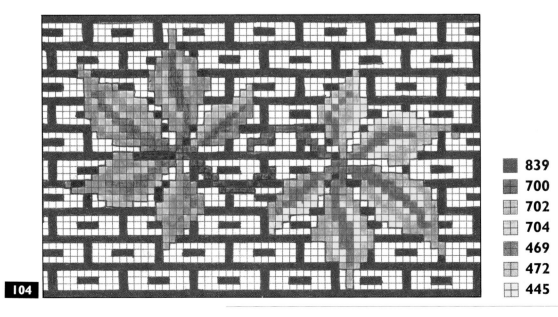

104

■	839
⊞	700
⊞	702
⊞	704
■	469
⊞	472
⊞	445

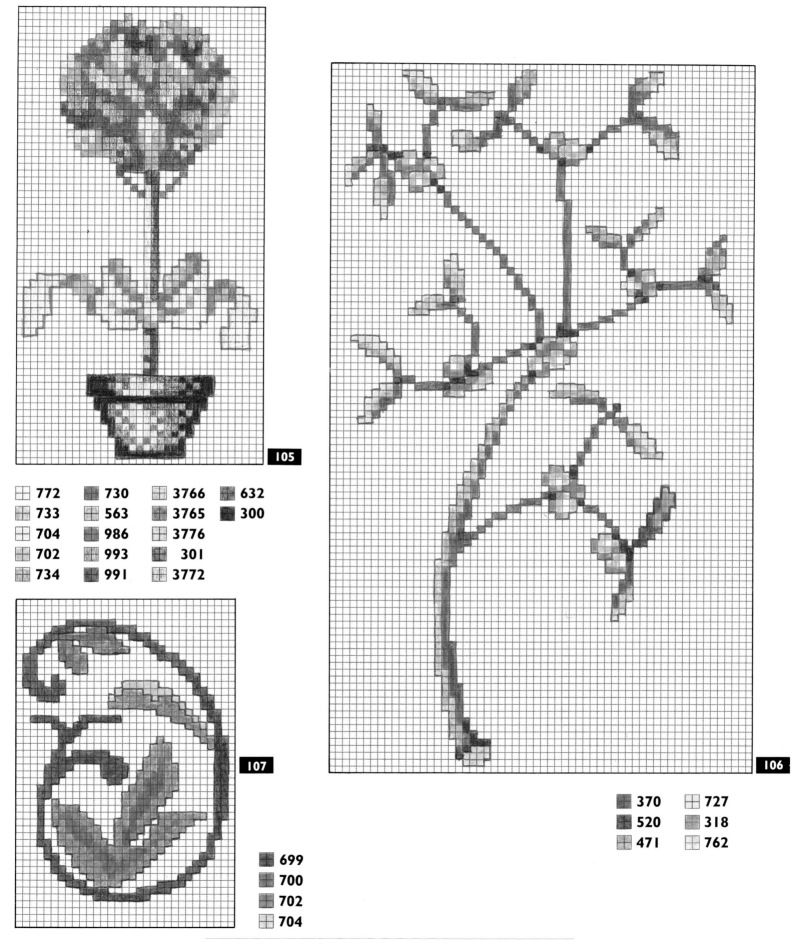

105

⊞ 772	▦ 730	⊞ 3766	▦ 632
⊞ 733	▦ 563	▦ 3765	▦ 300
⊞ 704	▦ 986	⊞ 3776	
▦ 702	▦ 993	▦ 301	
▦ 734	▦ 991	⊞ 3772	

107

▦ 699	
▦ 700	
▦ 702	
⊞ 704	

106

▦ 370	⊞ 727
▦ 520	▦ 318
⊞ 471	⊞ 762

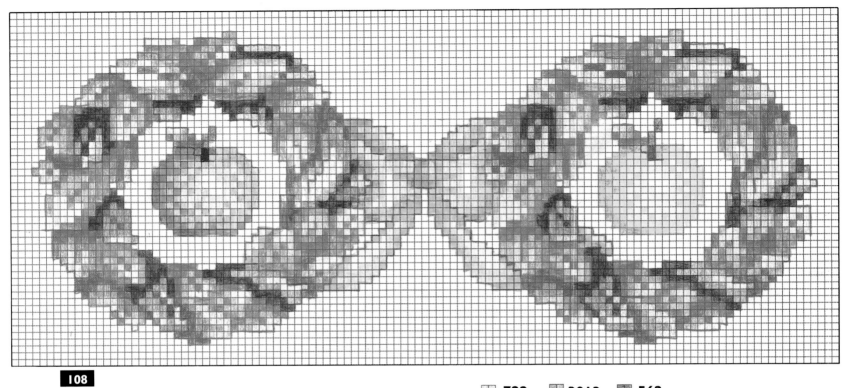

108

⊞ 722	⊞ 3013	⊞ 562
⊞ 721	⊞ 3012	⊞ 561
⊞ 720	⊞ 3011	⊞ 840
⊞ 353	⊞ 955	⊞ 838
⊞ 351	⊞ 913	⊞ 445
⊞ 350	⊞ 910	⊞ 444
⊞ 817	⊞ 564	⊞ 972

⊞ 472
⊞ 581
⊞ 369
⊞ 368
⊞ 319

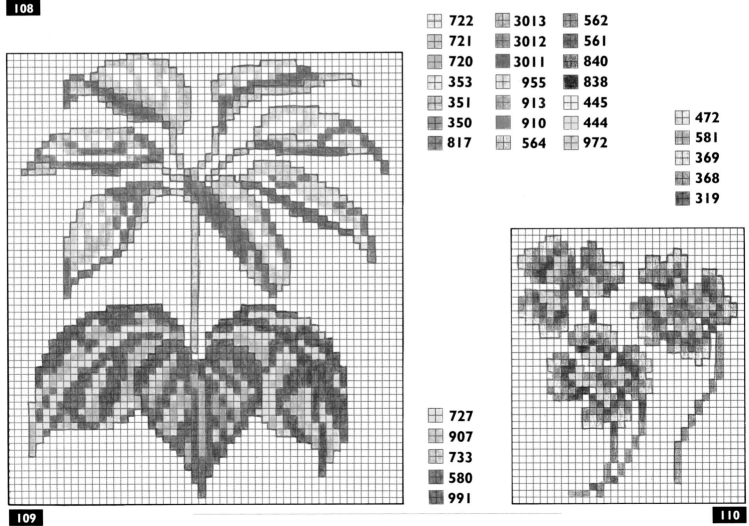

⊞ 727
⊞ 907
⊞ 733
⊞ 580
⊞ 991

109

110

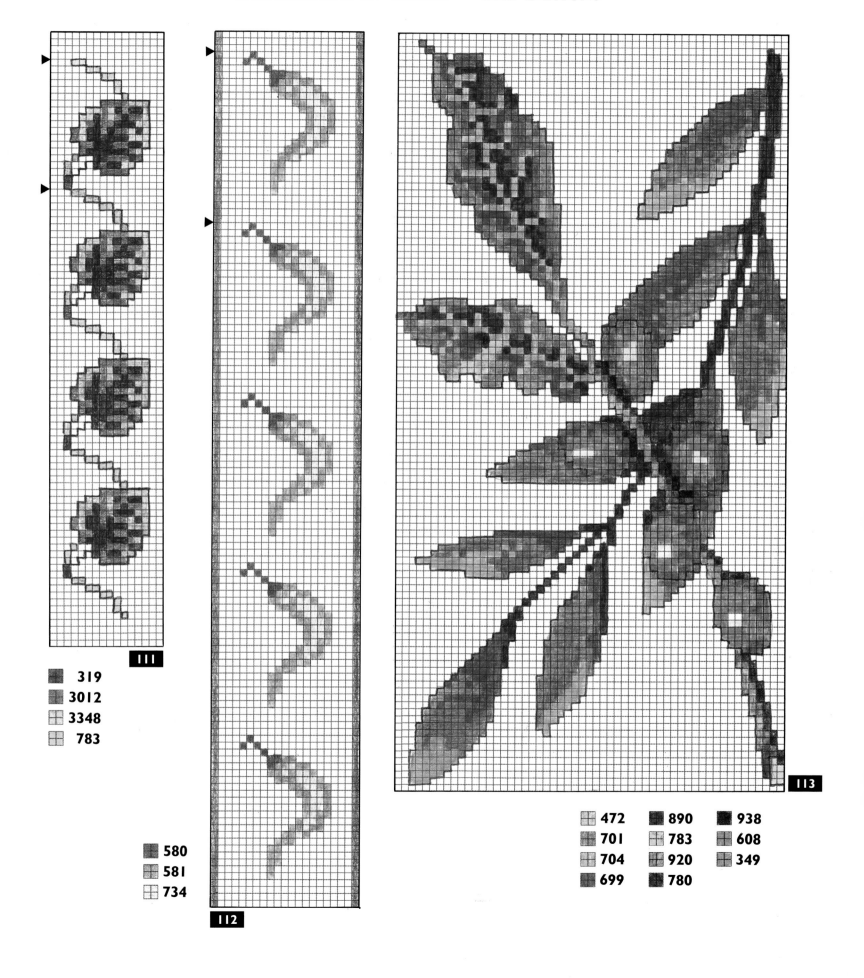

111

	319
	3012
	3348
	783

112

	580
	581
	734

113

	472		890		938
	701		783		608
	704		920		349
	699		780		

THE TECHNIQUE

Just as it is necessary to know the alphabet in order to write, it is necessary with cross stitch to know the two simple, basic components of its composition—two oblique crossover lines. Throughout the world, we can trace a period in the history of nearly every country where cross stitch has been employed. Embroidered items include furniture, in even the poorest of homes, linen, clothing and drapery. Beginner's efforts, made by children learning to work with needle and thread, are kept as mementos of childhood.

In essence cross stitch is a simple stitch that does not require other stitches to enhance it. It is used on its own in designs with either a single colour tone or a shaded colour effect. The only accompanying stitch that is sometimes used is backstitch: useful for outlining the edges of a design where a light coloured thread is used on a light coloured fabric, making it difficult to distinguish the design from the fabric. It is also used to emphasise a line of colour.

An equivalent style used in the Umbrian district of Italy is known as the 'Assisi Stitch'. It is most often stitched in blue or rust coloured thread and its usage originated in the town of Assisi. Cross stitch was used to fill the background of designs and a backstitch outline resulted in an effect that helped the central figures of the design, often birds or animals, to stand out quite prominently. Church decorations, monuments, signs and buildings, as well as laying, bas-relief, wrought iron and wood sculptures, provided a vast repertoire which, in turn, offered an inexhaustible supply of motifs for embroidery designs.

The cross stitch technique varies from country to country and often, whilst maintaining the basic characteristics of the stitch, there are variations in the length of the stitch. Examples include the varieties found in the Montenegro and Slavic countries.

When cross stitch is used on canvas, the entire background design needs to be filled in so that the colour of the canvas is not visible. This is not necessary on various other types of material but, above all, it is essential that the count and the weave of the fabric be even so that the crosses are identical in shape and size.

Once the motif has been chosen, it is important to plan the design on paper, especially if it is a complex one. You need to have the measurements in proportion in order to have a total picture of the finished design. Accurate measurements will help you to see any possible obstacles before you begin your work. Likewise, you should determine the size, both in length and width, of your chosen motif and then carefully tack the design onto the rectangle you have marked with coloured thread. This way you will be able to see if the design is ornate enough for the tablecloth, if one border is sufficient decoration for a curtain, or whether a table runner would look better with a double border. Initial calculation of the amount of space needed, whether for letters of the alphabet or small motifs of fruit, is a vital first step. If such a precaution is taken, there will be no unpleasant surprises with the finished pieces.

Corners for a border motif can easily be created using the following technique: place a mirror along the diagonal of the proposed corner so that the complete motif is reflected in the mirror. Copy this reflected image onto some graph paper, stitch by stitch, before continuing into the embroidery stage. If the chosen motifs are printed in colour only and you experience difficulty in distinguishing the colours, carefully transform the design into a sketch in black and white using conventional symbols to represent the various colours.

With the actual embroidery, it is best to work on the design first with all the required colours and tones, leaving the completion of the background until this is finished. It is also wise to complete a whole flower or a face of an animal before starting on the next motif to it. This will highlight problems at an early stage and allow the positioning of all the motifs so that the design is not cluttered.

THE STITCHES

ross stitch embroidery is an enjoyable technique. If the basic steps, which are few and uncomplicated, are followed, some incredible results can be achieved. For example, when working with a multi-coloured motif, take care with the reverse side of the fabric and keep the threads tidy. The threads should never be left too long and ends should be run back under the existing stitches.

Backstitch must also be executed according to the instructions in order to achieve a finished look which is aesthetically pleasing. Ideally, if you are working on a design in which the entire fabric needs to be filled in with cross stitch, work horizontally from left to right and vice versa. In cases where the outline is oblique, make a border using a half-cross stitch. This stitch is formed using a slanting or diagonal stitch and a small stitch that is perpendicular to the long one but meets at its centre.

When beginning or ending a thread, avoid the use of knots as they will show through the finished work. (Also, frequent washing and the passage of time may cause the knots to come undone.) To begin stitching, leave a length of thread at the back of the fabric, then work several stitches to secure it. To finish off a thread, weave the end under the last few stitches on the reverse side of the fabric. This method will give the embroidery a finished look on both the front and back of the work. This skilful method is ideal for curtains.

CROSS STITCH

  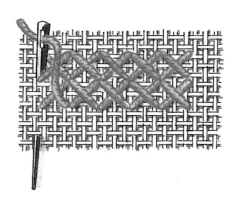

1. **From left to right:**
Work a row of diagonal stitches bringing the needle up at the bottom of the stitch first and then down at the top to complete the diagonal.

Then, without turning the work, complete the stitch by working a row of diagonal stitches moving in the other direction over the top of the first row, by bringing the needle up

at the bottom and then down at the top. To begin the next line, insert the needle vertically at the bottom of the stitch. On the back of the work there will be a sequence of vertical stitches.

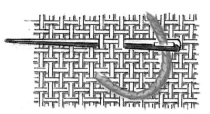

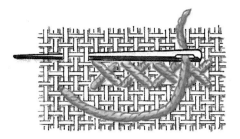

2. From right to left:
Work a diagonal stitch, bringing the needle up at the bottom of the stitch on the left and then inserting it diagonally to the right at the top.

Complete the cross stitch by repeating the diagonal stitch in the other direction: bring the needle up at the top of the stitch on the left and then insert the needle diagonally to the right at the bottom.

Continue in this manner, but make sure you leave enough space for the new stitch at the first step. Complete each stitch before proceeding to the next one.

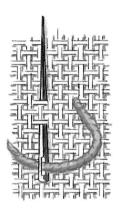
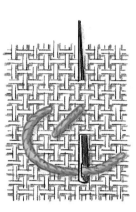
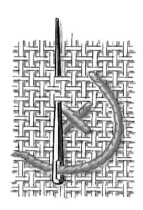
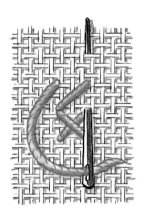
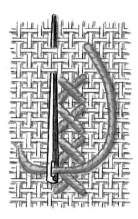

3. From bottom to top:
Bring the needle up at the top and work in a diagonal direction to the

bottom left corner. Complete by working the diagonal stitch from the top left corner to the bottom right

corner, then move to the next line in a vertical direction. Repeat the process for as many stitches as required.

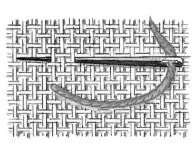

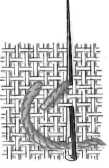
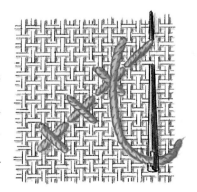

4. An upward diagonal direction:
Work the first complete cross as in Step

2, but finish with the needle at the top right hand corner. Work the next cross

stitch in same manner in a diagonal direction to the right and up.

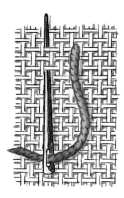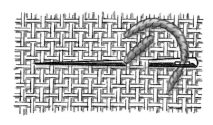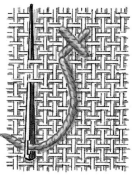

5. A downward diagonal direction:
Work the first cross as in Step 3, but

finish with the needle in the bottom left corner. Work the next cross stitch

in the same manner, left and down, in the diagonal direction.

DOUBLE RUNNING STITCH

6. A straight line
Work from right to left, making a row of evenly spaced stiches. Again

working from right to left, complete by working a second row, stitching in the spaces between the first row of stitches.

The result is a continuous line of stitches all the same size.

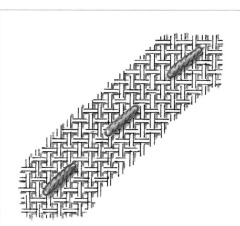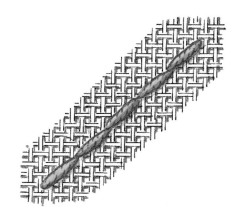

7. A diagonal line:
Beginning from the top right corner work a row of stitches the same size,

on both sides of the fabric, moving diagonally to the bottom left. To complete, work a second row, again

moving diagonally from top right. The result is a continuous line of stitches all the same size.

 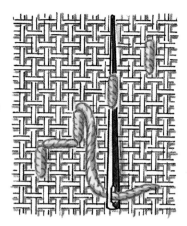 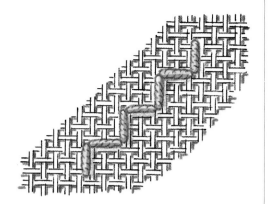

8. In a step manner:
Work a row of parallel, vertical lines, spaced so that a stitch the same size, in

both in horizontal and vertical directions, can be placed between them. To finish, work a second row,

parallel and horizontal, between the vertical stitches. This row should be the same size as the vertical stitches.

 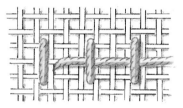 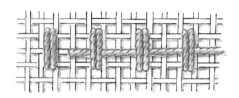

9. Backstitch for outlining:
Work stitches in any direction required to create a continuous line by bringing the thread up in front of the last stitch, leaving space for the new stitch, and then back into the fabric to fill in the space.

10. Beginning and finishing off a thread:
When you start stitching the first diagonals, make sure the thread end

is secured under the vertical lines on the reverse side. To finish, pass the thread under three or four of the double vertical stitches.

THE FABRICS

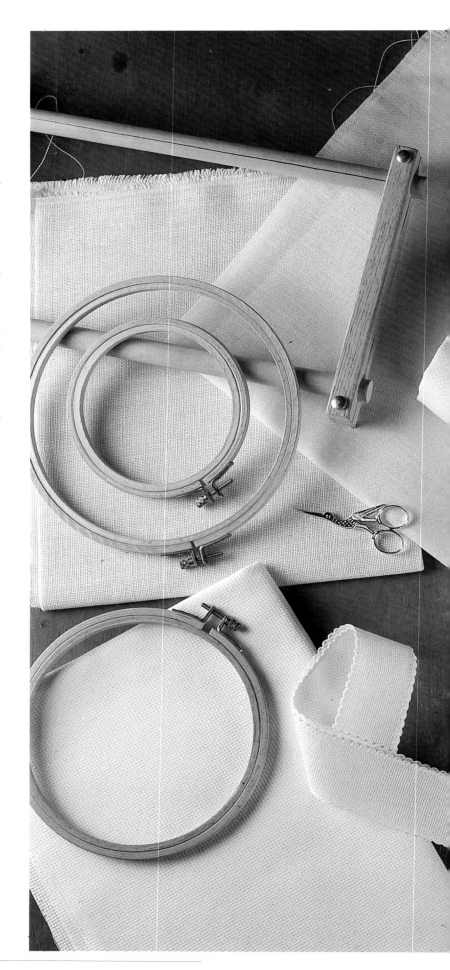

A fabric count is the number of threads per centimetre of fabric. For a perfect result, it is essential that it is absolutely even. The various kinds of Aida fabric are particularly good for cross stitch as the fabric count and the weave combine to form perfect squares. Pure linen is also good, providing 7 to 11 stitches per centimetre.

The Aida fabric in pure cotton is available in many widths and the stitch count for 10 cm varies from 72 to 60, to 55, to 44. The same motif, depending on the fabric, will require different measurements according to the stitch count of the fabric. The smaller the stitch count, the larger the finished design.

Pure linen with a regular fabric count suitable for cross stitch is also available in a variety of widths. It comes in white, unbleached or coloured forms. Linen with a larger fabric count (11 threads to 1 cm) allows for 55 cross stitches every 10 cm; linen with a smaller fabric count (7 threads to 1 cm) allows 35 cross stitches in every 10 cm if you take 2 x 2 fabric threads for each stitch. Naturally the number of the stitches possible will lessen if the threads are larger. Even with Aida fabric, a 2 x 2 square measurement will give very different sizes and results. A word of advice: because of the delicate nature of cross stitch designs, it is best to choose a fabric that will wear well with time and laundering. Bear in mind also, since pure cotton is as pleasing aesthetically as pure linen, it can be considered when choosing a suitable fabric.

Linen and Aida fabric have a regular fabric count and lend themselves perfectly to cross stitch. This even thread count allows a needle to slide through the material effortlessly. Coloured thread is likewise not a problem because the size of this thread is no thicker than the thread of the fabric. Obviously the dimensions of the embroidery vary depending on the type of fabric and the stitch count as can be seen with the rose design demonstrated on Aida fabric with 72, 55, and 94 stitch counts and Stranded cotton of 1, 2 and 3 threads.

THE YARNS

he DMC colour chart is based on Stranded and Pearl colours, and there are 398 different shades from which to choose the perfect tone of colour. There are at least eleven of each colour.

When choosing a design, yarn or fabric, other factors must be considered for the result you envisage. A thicker yarn, for example, will require a larger count in the fabric, and, vice versa, a thinner yarn will need a smaller count.

The DMC Stranded and Pearl threads have different features for the same colour. The Stranded is soft, flexible and luminous; comes in ready-made skeins and is made up of six fine threads that are perfect for filling in the background fabric on a completed embroidery design. Because of the nature of its composition, this yarn can be separated and used as 1, 2, 7 or 10 thread thickness. In other words, its usage can be adapted to even the lightest fabric and to every design.

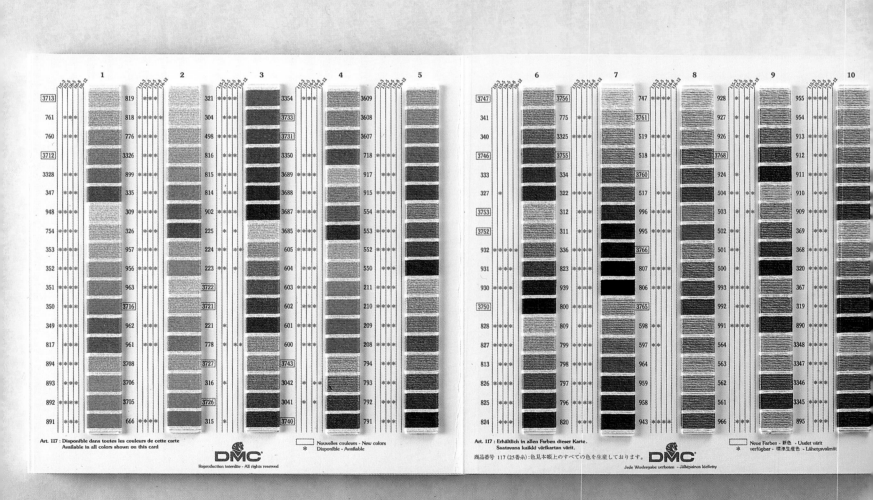

The DMC Pearl, on the other hand, is a shiny, glossy yarn, available in balls or skeins. It comes in two varieties: Number 5 in skeins and balls and Number 8 in balls. No. 8 is recommended for single-colour designs because the twist of the yarn can help give a brighter, clearer look to the outline of the embroidered fabric. No. 5 is suitable for embroidery on fabrics with a coarser count.

A final word of advice: whenever possible, it is always best to work on the darker colours of a design first, filling in the lighter colour last. This is because lighter shades seem to soil more readily and in so doing can spoil the overall effect of the finished design.

The entire range of embroidery yarns available from DMC offers over 398 varieties of combined and tinted shades. This broad choice should guarantee a tone that is just right for any design or piece of embroidery.

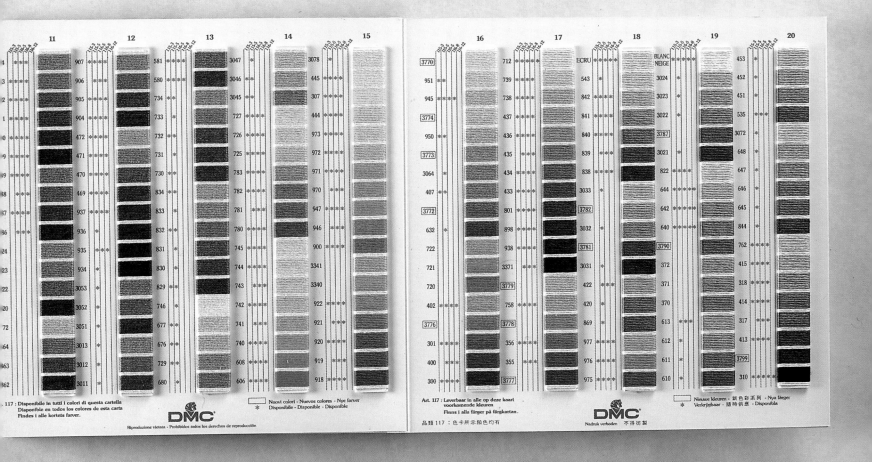

INSTRUCTIONS
FOR THE DESIGNS

Chapter by chapter the pages of this book unfold from shades of rose to shades of green like the colours of the rainbow. Each colour has inspirational photographs and examples of designs that have already been made up on paper grids. Also included is a number of designs shown only in chart form. These designs should help enrich your personal collection.

All the designs are numbered progressively throughout the book for easier identification. Below is a set of instructions for each one where the number of stitches both in width and height is given. The measurements are based on Aida fabric of 44, 55 and 60 stitches per 10 cm. This information will help you to choose the best type of fabric and yarn for the design. The page reference at the end of any instruction refers specifically to either a photograph of an existing embroidery or one of the designs.

Inspirations in
ROSE

1 The design is 95 stitches wide by 39 stitches high. If stitched on Aida with 44 stitches per 10 cm, it is 21.5 x 9 cm; on Aida with 55 or 60 stitches per 10 cm the dimensions are roughly 17 x 7 cm or 16 x 6.5 cm respectively.

2 The repeat motif indicated by the arrows is 28 stitches wide by 26 stitches high. It measures approximately 5.5 x 5 cm, 5 x 4.5 cm or 4.5 x 4.2 cm respectively on Aida with 44, 55 or 60 stitches per 10 cm.

3 The design repeat is 104 stitches high and 28 stitches wide. The measurements are approximately 23.6 x 6 cm, 19 x 5 cm and 17.5 x 4.5 cm on Aida with 44, 55 or 60 stitches per 10 cm.

4 The design is 59 stitches wide by 47 stitches high. Cross stitched on fabric with 44, 55 or 60 stitches per 10 cm, it measures approximately 13 x 11 cm, 11 x 8.5 or 10 x 8 cm respectively.

5 The motif repeat is 35 x 35 stitches. On Aida fabric with 44, 55 or 60 stitches per 10 cm, it measures approximately 8 x 8 cm, 6.5 x 6.5 cm or 6 x 6 cm respectively.

6 The motif repeat indicated by the arrows is 44 stitches across and 20 stitches high. On Aida with 44, 55 or 60 stitches per 10 cm. it is approximately 10 x 4.5 cm, 8 x 4 cm or 7.5 x 3.5 cm respectively. (See photograph on p. 30)

7 The design is 62 x 62 stitches. On Aida with 44, 55 or 60 stitches per 10 cm, it is approximately 14 x 14 cm, 11 x 11 cm or 10 x 10 cm respectively.

8 The design is 108 x 108 stitches. On Aida with 44, 55 or 60 stiches per 10cm it is approximately 24.5 x 24.5 cm, 20 x 20 cm or 18 x 18 cm respectively.

9 The design is 76 stitches wide and 72 stitches high. On Aida with 44, 55 or 60 stiches per 10 cm, it is approximately 17 x 16 cm, 14 x 13 cm or 13 x 12 cm respectively.

10 The repeat of the design between the arrows is 77 stitches across and 55 stitches high. On Aida with 44, 55 or 60 stiches per 10 cm, it is approximately 17.5 x 12.5 cm, 14 x 10 cm or 13 x 9 cm respectively. (See photograph on p. 15)

11 The repeat of the design between the arrows is 90 stitches high and 76 stitches across. On Aida with 44, 55 or 60 stiches per 10 cm, it is approximately 20.5 x 17 cm, 16 x 14 or 15 x 13 cm respectively.

12 The motif repeat between the arrows is 31 stitches high and 25 stitches wide. On Aida with 44, 55 or 60 stiches per 10 cm, it is approximately 7.5 x 5 cm, 5.5 x 4.5 cm or 5 x 4 cm respectively.

13 The design is 192 stitches wide and 131 stitches high. On Aida with 44, 55 or 60 stiches per 10 cm, it is approximately 43.5 x 30 cm, 35 x 24 cm or 32 x 22 cm respectively. (See photograph on p. 14)

Inspirations in
BLUE

14 The design is 80 x 82 stitches. On Aida with 44, 55 or 60 stiches per 10 cm, it is approximately 18 x 18.5 cm, 14.5 x 15 cm or 13.5 x 14 cm respectively. (See photograph on p. 29)

15 The motif repeat between the arrows is 27 stitches across and 25 stitches high. On Aida with 44, 55 or 60 stiches per 10 cm, it is approximately 6 x 5.5 cm, 5 x 4.5 cm or 4.5 x 4 cm respectively.

16 The design is 61 stitches across and 73 stitches high. On Aida with 44, 55 or 60 stiches per 10 cm, it is approximately 14 x 16.5 cm, 11 x 13.3 cm or 10 x 12 cm respectively.

17 The design is 102 x 102 stitches and on the above mentioned fabrics, it measures approximately 23 x 23 cm, 18.5 x 18.5 cm or 17 x 17 cm respectively.

18 The design is 53 x 64 stitches and on the above, it measures approximately 12 x 14.5 cm, 9.5 x 11.5 cm or 9 x 10.5 cm respectively.

19 The design is 24 x 49 stitches and on the above, it measures approximately 5.5 x 9 cm, 4.5 x 8.5 cm or 4 x 8 cm respectively.

20 The motif repeat is 24 x 33 stitches and it measures approximately 5.5 x 7.5 cm, 4.5 x 6 cm or 4 x 5.5 cm respectively.

21 The design is 45 x 58 stitches and it measures approximately 10 x 13 cm, 8 x 10.5 cm or 7.5 x 9.5 cm respectively.

22 The design is 104 x 79 stitches and it measures approximately 23.5 x 18 cm, 19 x 14.5 cm or 17.5 x 13 cm respectively.

23 The design repeat is 27 stitches wide and 38 stitches high and it measures approximately 6 x 8.5 cm, 5 x 7 cm or 4.5 x 6.5 cm respectively.

24 The design is 70 x 71 stitches and it measures approximately 16 x 16.1 cm, 12.7 x 13 cm or 11.6 x 12 cm respectively.

25 The design is 19 stitches across and the repeat is 13 stitches high. It measures approximately 4 x 3 cm, 3.5 x 2.5 cm or 3 x 2 cm respectively.

26 The design has a repeat of 99 stitches across and is 30 stitches high. It measures approximately 22.5 x 6.8 cm, 18 x 5.5 cm or 16.5 x 5 cm respectively. (See photograph on p. 29)

27 The design has a repeat of 56 stitches across and is 53 stitches high. It measures approximately 13 x 12 cm, 10 x 9.5 cm or 9.5 x 9 cm respectively.

28 The design is 37 x 29 stitches and it measures approximately 8.5 x 6.5 cm, 7 x 6 cm or 6 x 5 cm respectively.

29 The design has a repeat of 24 stitches across and is 33 stitches high. It measures approximately 5.3 x 7.5 cm, 4.3 x 6 or 4 x 5.5 cm respectively.

30 The design has a repeat of 27 stitches high and 42 stitches across. It measures approximately 6 x 10.5 cm, 5 x 7.5 cm or 4.5 x 7 cm respectively.

31 The design has a repeat of 48 stitches across and is 32 stitches high. It measures approximately 11 x 7.5 cm, 9 x 6 cm or 8 x 5.5 cm respectively.

32 The design repeat is 9 stitches wide and is 5 stitches high. It measures approximately 1 cm, almost 1 cm or 8 mm respectively.

33 The design repeat is 48 x 40 stitches and it measures approximately 11 x 10 cm, 9 x 7 cm or 8 x 6.5 cm respectively.

34 The design is 38 x 49 stitches and it measures approximately 8.5 x 11 cm, 7 x 9 cm or 6.5 x 8 cm respectively.

35 The design is 31 x 52 stitches and it measures approximately 7 x 12 cm, 5.5 x 9.5 cm or 5 x 8.5 cm respectively.

36 The design repeat is 44 stitches across and is 52 stitches high. It measures approximately 10 x 12 cm, 8 x 9.5 cm or 7.5 x 8.5 cm respectively.

37 The design repeat is 13 stitches across and is 22 stitches high. It measures approximately 3 x 5 cm, 2.5 x 4 cm or 2 x 3.5 cm respectively.

38 The design is 33 stitches high and the repeat is 30 stitches across. It measures approximately 7.5 x 7 cm, 6 x 5.5 cm or 5.5 x 5 cm respectively.

39 The design is 62 x 34 stitches and it measures approximately 14 x 8 cm, 11 x 6 cm or 10 x 5.5 cm respectively.

40 The design is 137 x 136 stitches and it measures approximately 30 x 30 cm, 22 x 22 cm or 13 x 13 cm respectively. (See photograph on p. 28)

41 The design is 203 x 150 stitches and it measures approximately 46 x 34 cm, 37 x 27 cm or 34 x 25 cm respectively. (See photograph on pp. 32–33)

42 The design is 25 wide and the repeat is 33 stitches high. It measures approximately 5.5 x 7.5 cm, 4.5 x 6 cm or 4 x 5.5 cm respectively.

Inspirations in
VIOLET

43 The design is 17 stitches across and the repeat is 16 stitches high. It measures approximately 4 x 4 cm, 3 x 3 cm or 2 x 2 cm respectively.

44 The design is 59 stitches wide and 93 stitches high. It measures approximately 13.5 x 21 cm, 11 x 17 cm or 10 x 15.5 cm respectively.

45 The design repeat is 43 stitches wide and 40 stitches high. It measures approximately 10 x 9 cm, 8 x 7 cm or 7 x 6.5 cm respectively.

46 The design is 17 stitches across and the repeat is 26 stitches high. It measures approximately 4 x 6 cm, 3 x 5 cm or 2.8 x 4.5 cm respectively.

47 The design (to be turned and repeated 4 times to complete the wreath) is 74 stitches wide and 78 stitches high. It measures approximately 33.5 x 35.5 cm, 27 x 28.5 cm or 24.5 x 26 cm respectively. (See photograph on page 114)

48 The design repeat is 38 x 38 stitches and it measures approximately 8.5 x 8.5 cm, 7 x 7 cm or 6.5 x 6.5 cm respectively.

49 The design repeat is 58 x 58 stitches and it measures approximately 13 x 13 cm, 10.5 x 10.5 cm or 9.5 x 9.5 cm respectively.

50 The design is 103 stitches wide and 57 stitches high. It measures approximately 23.5 x 13 cm, 19 x 10.5 cm or 17 x 9.5 cm respectively.

51 The design is 31 stitches across and 72 stitches high. It measures approximately 7 x 16.5 cm, 5.5 x 13 cm or 5 x 12 cm respectively.

52 The design is 50 stitches across and 44 stitches high. It measures approximately 11.5 x 10 cm, 9 x 8 cm or 8.5 x 7.5 cm respectively.

53 The design repeat is 39 stitches high and is 31 stitches across. It measures approximately 9 x 7 cm, 7 x 5.5 cm or 6.5 x 5 cm respectively.

54 The design is 142 x 142 stitches and it measures approximately 31 x 31 cm, 16 x 16 cm or 14 x 14 cm respectively.

55 The design is 39 stitches across and 62 stitches high. It measures approximately 9 x 14 cm, 7 x 11 cm or 6.5 x 10 cm respectively.

Inspirations in
YELLOW

56 The design repeat is 32 stitches across and 48 stitches high. It measures approximately 7 x 11 cm, 6 x 9 cm or 5.5 x 8 cm respectively. (See photograph on pp. 60–61)

57 The design is 64 stitches across and 28 stitches high. It measures approximately 14.5 x 6.5 cm, 11.5 x 5 cm or 10.5 x 4.5 cm respectively.

58 The design is 43 stitches across and 60 stitches high. It measures approximately 10 x 13.5 cm, 8 x 11 cm or 7 x 10 cm respectively.

59 The design is 102 stitches wide and 110 stitches high. It measures approximately 23 x 25 cm, 18.5 x 20 cm or 17 x 18.5 cm respectively. (See photograph on pp. 62–63)

60 The design repeat is 44 stitches wide and 39 stitches high. It measures approximately 10 x 9 cm, 8 x 7 cm or 7.5 x 6.5 cm respectively.

61 The design repeat is 25 stitches across and 16 stitches high. It measures approximately 5.5 x 3.5 cm, 4.5 x 3 cm or 4 x 2.5 cm respectively.

62 The design repeat is 64 x 32 stitches and it measures approximately 14.5 x 7 cm, 11.5 x 6 cm or 10.5 x 5.5 cm respectively.

63 The design repeat is 49 x 39 stitches and it measures approximately 11 x 9 cm, 9 x 7 cm or 8 x 6.5 cm respectively.

64 The design is 40 x 64 stitches and it measures approximately 9 x 14.5 cm, 7 x 11.5 cm or 6.5 x 10.5 cm respectively.

65 The design is 52 x 52 stitches and it measures approximately 12 x 12 cm,

9.5 x 9.5 cm, or 8.5 x 8.5 cm respectively.

66 The design is 180 x 140 stitches and it measures approximately 41 x 32 cm, 33 x 26 cm or 30 x 23.5 cm respectively. (see photographs on pp. 64–65).

Inspirations in
ORANGE

67 The design repeat is 18 x 32 stitches and it measures approximately 4 x 7 cm, 3.5 x 6 cm or 3 x 5.5 cm respectively.

68 The design is 61 stitches across and 102 stitches high. It measures approximately 14 x 23 cm, 11 x 18.5 cm or 10 x 17 cm respectively.

69 The design repeat is 29 x 44 stitches and it measures approximately 6.5 x 10 cm, 5.5 x 8.5 cm or 5 x 7.5 cm respectively.

70 The design repeat is 51 x 35 stitches and it measures approximately 11.5 x 8 cm, 9 x 6.5 cm or 8.5 x 6 cm respectively.

71 The design repeat is 15 x 16 stitches and it measures approximately 3.5 x 3.5 cm, 3 x 3 cm or 2.5 x 2.5 cm respectively.

72 The design is 75 x 73 stitches and it measures approximately 17 x 16 cm, 13.5 x 13 cm or 12.5 x 12 cm respectively. (See photographs on pp. 74–75)

73 The design is 69 x 55 stitches and it measures approximately 15.5 x 12.5

cm, 12.5 x 10 cm or 11.5 x 9 cm respectively. (See photographs on pp. 74–75)

74 The design repeat is 26 x 31 stitches and it measures approximately 6 x 7 cm, 5 x 5.5 cm or 4.5 x 5 cm respectively. (See photograph on p. 81)

75 The design repeat is 19 x 11 stitches and it measures approximately 4 x 2.5 cm, 3.5 x 2 cm or 3 x 1.8 cm respectively.

76 The design repeat is 31 x 77 stitches and it measures approximately 7 x 17.5 cm, 5.5 x 14.5 cm or 5 x 13 cm respectively.

77 The design is 69 x 58 stitches and it measures approximately 15.5 x 13 cm, 12.5 x 10.5 cm or 11.5 x 9.5 cm respectively. (See photograph on p. 80)

78 The design is 33 x 53 stitches and it measures approximately 7.5 x 12 cm, 6 x 9.5 cm or 5.5 x 9 cm respectively. (See photograph on p. 80)

79 The design repeat is 48 x 31 stitches and it measures approximately 11 x 7 cm, 9 x 5.5 cm or 8 x 5 cm respectively.

80 The design is 26 x 41 stitches and it measures approximately 6 x 9 cm, 4.5 x 7.5 cm or 4 x 7 cm respectively.

81 The design is 70 x 146 stitches and it measures approximately 16 x 33 cm, 12.5 x 26.5 cm or 11.5 x 24 cm respectively. (See photographs on pp. 78–79)